Back Roads of Southern Spain

25 great car trips around Andalusia

by David Baird

Published in September 2002 by Santana Books.
© David Baird 2002
Designed by Andrea Carter
Map of Andalusia by Estinca Ingeniería Cartográfica

"**Back Roads of Southern Spain**"
is published by Ediciones Santana S.L.,
Apartado 422, Fuengirola 29640 (Málaga), Spain.
Tel. 952 485 838. Fax 952 485 367.
E-mail: info@santanabooks.com
www.santanabooks.com

Printed and bound in Spain by Gráficas San Pancracio S.L.,
Polígono Industrial San Luis, Málaga.

Depósito Legal: MA-1.363/2002
ISBN 84-89954-23-2

CONTENTS

Introduction

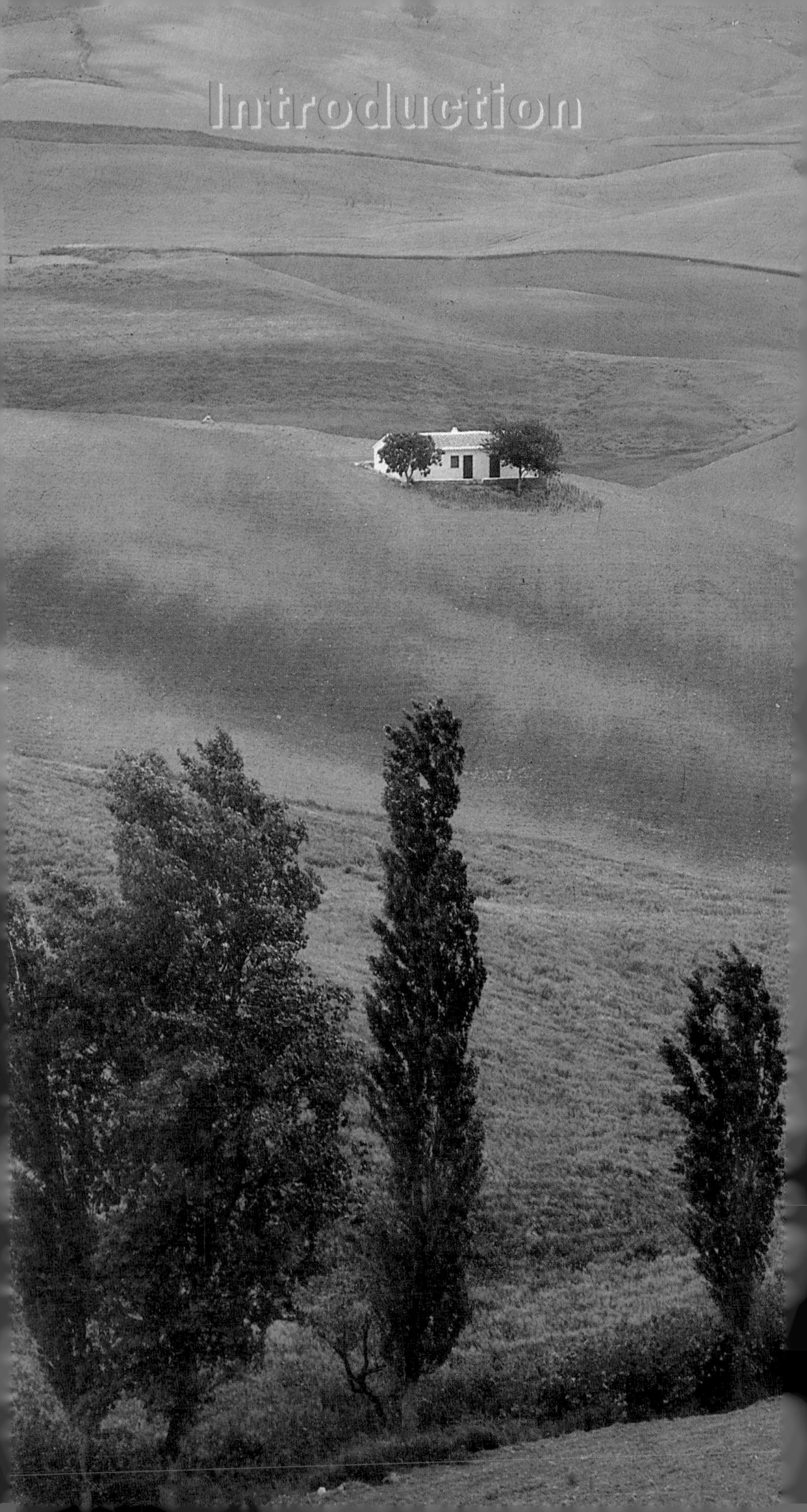

"THERE IS, SIR, A GOOD DEAL OF SPAIN THAT HAS NOT BEEN PERAMBULATED. I WOULD HAVE YOU GO THITHER; A MAN OF INFERIOR TALENTS TO YOURS MAY FURNISH US WITH USEFUL OBSERVATIONS OF THAT COUNTRY."
– Samuel Johnson's advice to Boswell, as quoted by Richard Ford.

Church at Olvera

Around every corner in Southern Spain you will find something to surprise you, whether it's a lively local fiesta, a breath-taking panorama, a dramatically located village, a soaring eagle - or a friendly wayside inn. Beyond the coastal resorts and the great cities, rural Spain awaits your discovery.

This book is designed for those who want to get off the beaten track and visit places where many tourists never think to venture. Exploring the byways will take you to trout streams and hiking trails, to lush vineyards and arid desert, to towns steeped in history and troglodyte villages, to both the Frying Pan and the Ice Cube of Andalusia. Experience Andalusia's countless attractions close-up.

We tell you how to get there in 25 excursions. Apart from route details and background about the places visited, you will find highly practical information about the most important sights, possible overnight stops and where to eat. And we have included driving hints, basic vocabulary and fiesta dates.

INFORMATION

Addresses are given of tourist information offices along the routes. Municipal and provincial authorities as well as the Junta de Andalucía provide a useful service, giving out maps, brochures, booklets in several languages, and information about coming events.

Tourist information about the region, including a hotel reservation service, is available at the officially sponsored website (www.andalucia.org). For basic tourist information (in Spanish, English, French and German) about Spain in general, including useful addresses and telephone numbers, you can call 901 300 600 between 8am and 10pm seven days a week. The call is charged at a reduced rate. A similar service is offered for Andalusia at 901 200 020.

VISITING HOURS

National monuments and museums are usually closed on Mondays. Unless otherwise stated, churches are usually only open for services, most often in the evening. However, ask around as the local priest or caretaker may be available to give access. Citizens of the European Union have free entrance to a number of sights where non-Europeans must pay. Check visiting times with tourist offices as these can vary, especially during summer when monuments tend to open later in the afternoon.

TRANSPORT

Travelling by car or motorcycle gives you the independence to reach remoter corners. However, public transport is well developed – just allow sufficient time to make connections. Trains run between major centres, but comfortable, air-conditioned buses are more frequent and usually cheaper. There may be only one bus a day to smaller villages. Cycling can be fun, but it is only for the fit because of the mountainous character of the country and it is definitely not recommended in summer heat.

ON THE ROAD

Communications across Spain have been vastly improved and four-lane highways (autovías) link major cities in Andalusia. But this guide is not for those in a hurry. The routes stick to less-frequented minor roads. These are usually well paved and you never have to hit dirt unless you want to - unsealed tracks through scenic areas are indicated for the more adventurous. When calculating travelling time, remember that many routes wind through mountainous territory so that progress can be slower than expected.

Driving in Spain is on the right and traffic entering from the right has priority unless otherwise signalled. Particularly on country routes, expect to encounter vehicles hogging the centre of the road, often on bends. Compensate for happy-go-lucky local motorists by being extra cautious. Don't take road signs as gospel, e.g. sometimes indications that it is safe to overtake should be taken with a pinch of salt. Drivers and passengers are required to use seat belts.

Motorcycles without lights, mules and other livestock can be hazards at night. The law requires motorcyclists to wear crash helmets, although this is often not observed. Be warned: teenage riders may try to overtake on the inside.

If stopped by a Civil Guard highway patrol, maintain good humour and don't argue. They can impose extremely heavy, on-the-spot fines for driving offences. Speed traps are common. The speed limit in urban areas is usually 30mph (50kph). On main roads the limit is usually 50mph (80km) to 62mph (100kph). On auto routes the limit is 75mph (120km).

Petrol stations are much more numerous than a few years ago, but can be sparse in country areas and they usually close at night. Prices vary little between different gas stations. Leadless petrol is widely available, Euro super (95 octane) and Super plus (98 octane).

If driving your own vehicle, bring the car documents, international insurance and a bail bond in case of accident, an international driving licence (although for short stays by EEC visitors your national licence should be sufficient), spare car light bulbs, fan belt and two red warning triangles.

MAPS

Michelin's map of Southern Spain (number 446) is recommended as a guide to Andalusian roads. It includes an index of places with map coordinates. Firestone T-29 offers a larger-scale view of the Costa del Sol and hinterland and includes maps of Antequera, Fuengirola, Granada, Málaga, Marbella, Ronda and Torremolinos. Unfortunately, it badly needs updating and can be highly misleading. The annual Campsa guide has good foldout maps of all Spain, plus tourist and gastronomic information.

WORTH KNOWING

- Where possible, avoid making excursions at weekends and during peak holiday periods, particularly Easter week, as sights and hotels can get very crowded. Midweek, hotel rates are often lower. Ask about special discounts for over-60s and students.

- Each of Andalusia's eight provinces has a tourist village, built in traditional style and funded by the regional government. These *villas turísticas* offer comfortable accommodation in tranquil surroundings at reasonable prices. Each unit usually has a livingroom, fireplace and kitchenette. More information: www.naturahoteles.com

- Road signs can be misleading. Sometimes, even though you are warned "Carretera cerrada", roads are open - nobody has bothered to remove the old sign. Other signs are serious understatements *Curva* may mean several hairpin bends, Gravilla suelta may herald a deep pit in the road.

- In remoter areas decent eating places are few and far between. But some of your most memorable meals will be picnics. Fruit, ham, cheese and wine are always obtainable at village stores. Remember to bring drinking cups, a corkscrew and a knife.

- The months of April, May and June and September and October are ideal for touring. In winter, while the sun often shines strongly, the weather is often colder and wetter than many visitors expect, particularly in mountainous areas, so bring a range of clothing. Light clothing is essential in summer when Southern Spain can be very hot, especially in the interior.

- Casual dress is acceptable almost anywhere. But dress appropriately when sightseeing. Anything may go in tourist resorts, but elsewhere locals have little respect for sun-blistered, half-dressed visitors wandering their streets and scanty gear is definitely out when visiting places of worship. You only require formal dress for better-class restaurants and social occasions such as weddings.

- Information boards marking the start of many walks in Andalusia are not always reliable. Some estimates seem to have been made with Olympic champions in mind and walks can take up to double the time suggested. Make sure you have reliable maps and a good walkers' guide - there are several in English and Spanish, including "Walking in Andalucía", published by Santana Books.

SECURITY

Although country areas are much safer than cities, commonsense precautions should be observed. Never leave valuables or documents in an unattended car at any time. When staying overnight, take all baggage into the hotel. If possible, park your car in a garage or a guarded car park. If you leave your car in the street, expose the boot interior if possible so that it is obvious there is nothing worth taking. Unofficial parking attendants - dubbed "gorillas" by the locals - may ask you for money. The safest course is to give them something.

If driving through Seville, do not leave anything of value within view. The *semaforazo* is a local custom; youths smash the windows of out-of-town cars at traffic lights, grab anything in sight, then escape by motorcycle. Leave valuables, your passport and other documents in the hotel safe. Make photocopies if you want to carry identification.

Look for three distinct police forces: the "municipales" (blue uniforms, peaked caps), employed by the local council for minor tasks such as bill collection and controlling traffic; National Police (dark blue uniforms), concerned with crime prevention and investigation; Civil Guards (olive-green uniforms, their distinctive patent leather tricorn hats have been relegated to ceremonial occasions), crime prevention in small towns and rural areas. National police stations (comisarías) in tourist areas generally have report forms in several languages.

EATING OUT

Value-for-money eating places abound throughout Andalusia and standards have risen considerably in recent years. Although you are unlikely to find fancy restaurants on the back roads, the region has awakened to the importance of good cuisine and you can now dine in style on local dishes, some with clear Arabic influence. Remember that Spaniards take meals late, lunch any time between 2 and 4pm, dinner after 9pm. Tapas (snacks) are usually available at all hours.

The venta, or roadside inn, is a great Spanish institution. They are cheap, cheerful and offer very good value, which is why you will find quite a number recommended in this book. Decor is basic and a television may be blasting away in one corner to keep diners properly entertained. Nobody pays any attention to it as they are too busy enjoying substantial meals at bargain prices.

The best value is usually the menú del día, a hearty three-course meal for around 6 euros. There may be no written menu so, if there's a language barrier, ask to see what is cooking and point at what you want. Payment is usually by cash.

In most of the restaurants (as opposed to ventas) listed, expect to pay around 15-18 euros per person for a three-course meal without wine. Except for cheaper establishments, most places now accept credit cards, nearly always Visa and MasterCard, less frequently Diners and American Express.

If you cannot find a place billing itself as a venta or restaurant, look for a bar or mesón (a fancy name for a bar serving food). Most serve tasty tapas. Ask for a ración if you want a plateful.

WHERE TO STAY

Travelling through the back country used to be a spartan business. Tales of sagging mattresses and astonishing toilets abounded. No longer. Andalusia has hundreds of small hotels in rural areas offering modern comfortable accommodation, usually with en suite bathrooms. Heating and hot water are now normal features.

Old mansions and farmhouses have been converted into rural hotels and some are truly stylish and luxurious. In addition, there are many casas rurales available for rent by groups for longer stays. These are usually converted farmhouses of varying degrees of comfort. Inquire at tourist information offices and town halls.

A blue plaque outside hotels indicates the official rating. At the bottom end of the market, *P* stands for pension or hostal. Remember that pension and hotel star ratings only take into account the amenities provided, not the quality of the service or atmosphere. Prices run from around 24 euros a night at a simple pension to around 120 euros in a parador.

In this guide, as prices can vary depending on the year and season, the rates listed are only approximate. The price for two people staying overnight in a double room, including taxes, is indicated by a euro symbol (€). Breakfast is often included in the price.

€ under 40 euros

€€ 40-60 euros

€€€ 60-90 euros

€€€€ over 90 euros

It is worth inquiring at travel agencies about special deals, as many discounts are available for larger hotels, including paradors. Advance booking is essential. The Junta de Andalucía (the regional government) publishes a useful annual guide to all accommodation, including apartments and campsites. It is available in tourist information offices.

Particularly handy for users of this guide is a companion volume published by Santana Books. "Small Hotels and Inns of Andalucía" by Guy Hunter-Watts lists details of more than 100 places to stay, selected for their charm and value for money.

LET US KNOW
We welcome your help in keeping this guidebook as up to date as possible. If you come across any changes, if you discover a restaurant worth recommending or a hotel with a special appeal, please let us know. We shall take it into account and give you a mention when preparing the next edition.

A corrida in the Ronda Plaza de Toros

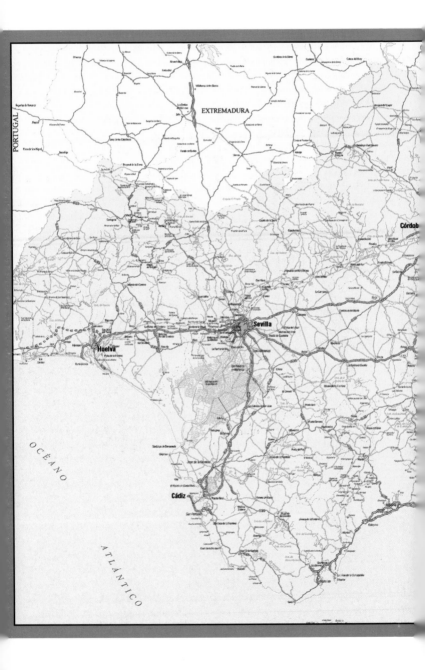

CASTILLA LA MANCHA

MURCIA

Jaén

Granada

Almería

MAR MEDITERRÁNEO

In the Steps of Caesar

Gaucin – the archetypal Andalusian village

RIDE THE RIDGES OF THE BACK COUNTRY WHERE HEROIC WARRIORS ONCE FOUGHT OVER HILLTOP FORTRESSES, CANNON-BALLS WERE FORGED TO BESIEGE GIBRALTAR AND JULIUS CAESAR SOUGHT A CURE FOR DANDRUFF OR WORSE. THIS EXCURSION IS A GOOD INTRODUCTION TO THE WONDERS OF ANDALUSIA.

AREA: West Málaga province and southern Cádiz province
ROUTE: Estepone→Casares→Gaucín→Jimena→Castellar→Estepona
DISTANCE: 130 kilometres

1   In the steps of Caesar

From the N340, nine kilometres west of Estepona, turn inland to take the MA546 to Casares. You snake upwards past cattle pastures, then cork oaks and fire-seared pines in the foothills of the Sierra Bermeja.

Topping a rise, 14 kilometres from the coast, abruptly you encounter Casares (pop. 3000), a village apparently designed for picture postcards. It looks as though somebody has played dice with hundreds of white cubes. They spill over a rocky saddle and up the facing slopes to jostle the battlements of an Arab castle.

Several restaurants serving local dishes offer this panorama from their dining rooms or terraces. Try codornices en salsa verde (quail in green sauce).

Look for a sharp left-hand turn to bring you into the village. Don't try to drive through the narrow streets. Instead, park your car at the first small square and walk up to the Plaza de España, with its bars and pensions. White doves flutter about the fountain.

Here stands a statue of Blas Infante, regarded as the Father of Andalusia. He was a notary, born in Casares, who led an Andalusian nationalist movement, until he was executed by Franco's rebels at the start of the Civil War. The town hall is preparing the house where he was born, 51 Calle Carrera, as a museum and cultural centre.

Eventually you come out on top of the town, 400 metres above sea level. Here is a derelict church, sacked during the Civil War, and Casares cemetery. And here is the old fortress, offering one of the great views.

A fresh breeze usually blows over the heights. Look out for peregrine falcons and kestrels riding the wind and gaze out towards the coast, the Rock of Gibraltar and the mountains of Morocco. Casares history goes back at least 3000 years and waves of invaders broke against this gaunt, rocky pinnacle. One version has it that it was named after Julius Caesar.

Pedro the Cruel seized the fortress from the Moors in the 14th century and, after an unsuccessful 16th-century revolt by the

Moriscos, hundreds of rebel prisoners were hurled from this crag into the ravine. Some nasty things also happened more recently, during the Spanish Civil War.

Continuing on the road that loops around Casares, you reach the A377. You can return to the coast by turning left, passing hills topped with whirling windmills to reach Manilva 24 kilometres away. This area produces delicious eating grapes and every year in the first week of September a riotous wine festival is held.

Just before Manilva, where trucks rumble out of a quarry, a road leads steeply downhill to the Manilva River. At the bottom turn left under the new auto route bridge, following a dusty track. After 0.8 kilometres, before the San Adolfo chapel, park on an open space near the Baños Romanos.

You can bathe in cool sulphurous waters beneath ancient arches, just like Julius Caesar – in 61BC he allegedly cured a skin infection here. It could be a delightful spot, but only when the local authority cleans up the sadly neglected surrounds.

For a longer excursion, instead of running downhill from Casares, turn right on the A377 to Gaucín. Soon you see the splendidly situated village with its 13th-century castle spearing the skyline. In or near Gaucín's castle Guzmán El Bueno, hero of Tarifa, died in battle with the Moors in 1309.

At Number 8 on San Juan de Dios street, an old-style fonda, the Nacional, no longer rents rooms but serves hearty meals. It has catered for weary travellers since 1868. In the 19th century, when it was known as the Hotel Inglés, it welcomed many a British military type travelling between Gibraltar and Ronda. Smugglers carrying tobacco from Gibraltar were also among the clients.

Ask to see the original registry, so thumbed that a photocopy has been made. It includes the remarks of both testy and well-pleased visitors. "The saddles were invented by the Inquisition," growled one, while another commented "capital cooking and the best wine we have had in Spain".

Within the castle walls a church shelters the much-venerated Santo Niño Dios. This image of the Holy Child is carried in procession through the village in the first week of September every year.

Expatriate North Europeans have settled in force around Gaucín, as they have at the next town, Jimena de la Frontera. We head southwest on the A369, which soon starts to descend through hilly pastures where cattle with wickedly-pronged horns peer out from amid the oak trees.

Straggling down a hillside below a ruined castle, Jimena was in the forefront of the battle between Castilian forces and the kingdom of Granada for two centuries. A labyrinthine route through somewhat scruffy narrow streets takes you up to the castle – nervous drivers suffering from claustrophobia may wish to abstain. Below the castle an information office is splendidly housed in the old Misericordia church.

At the southern entrance to town, inhabitants take their evening stroll and stalls are erected for the Friday market on the Paseo. In the middle of this esplanade is a neo-classical tower, all that remains of Santa María La Coronada church.

Bombs and cannonballs used in the 1782 siege of Gibraltar were made at the Reales Fábricas de Artillería, an artillery factory with blast furnaces by the Río Hozgarganta. Remains can be seen, including a 650-metre canal that carried water to power the bellows.

Below Jimena off the A369 is the Estación de Jimena, past which runs the Algeciras-Ronda rail line. This brilliant piece of work was built in the 1890s by English engineer John Morrison, backed by a wealthy financier, Sir Alexander Henderson. The halts along the line have similar architecture to those of rural English stations.

Here too is a 15th-century Franciscan monastery that shelters the Virgen de Los Angeles carved – according to legend – by St Luke.

Drive down the irrigated river valley, passing orange groves and cork-processing plants. A sharp right-hand turn takes you eight kilometres up a sinuous road to Castellar de la Frontera. Wild boar and deer roam slopes thick with holm and cork oaks, ash and oleander. After passing the Venta Jarandilla – venison or wild boar could be on the menu – you sight the Guadarranque reservoir below on our left.

Castellar's ramparts loom above boulder-strewn slopes. Goats graze the area, stripping leaves from trees and sometimes trotting across the rooftops of the houses nestled among the rocks. Young Britons and Germans are among the residents.

Leave your car below the castle entrance, near Al Andalús bar and an information point (not always open). From here, 250 metres above sea level, you look towards the Strait and Gibraltar crouching on guard.

Pigeons flutter about the restored towers of the castle, once a ducal residence. Walk up a ramp and through archways to enter this village fortress which until comparatively recently closed its gate every night as in feudal times.

Built in the 13th century, Castellar was finally captured from the Moors in 1434 by Juan de Saavedra, lord of neighbouring Jimena. A nephew became Count of Castellar, to be succeeded later by the Duques de Medinaceli who ruled over La Almoraima estate, covering 16,000 hectares.

The hardness of the life here finally persuaded the authorities to offer the 2000 inhabitants land and housing below in the valley in 1971. Nearly everybody decamped and Castellar became a ghost town.

Hippies moved in, but now many of the houses have been bought by outsiders and a number converted into rental accommodation. Even so, there's a spooky air about these silent streets occupied only by stray cats.

A road runs beyond Castellar but is virtually impassable, so you return to the junction with the A369. Here stands an unusual hotel in extensive grounds. La Almoraima was constructed as a convent with money obtained from fines levied on the unfortunate Castellar folk by their feudal lords. Later it became a hunting lodge for the Medinaceli family.

1 In the steps of Caesar

The spacious new village of Castellar is somewhat soulless. But in the first week of May it is filled with picturesque movement. Thousands arrive to pay homage to Santa Cristo de La Almoraima, a much-venerated image of Christ on the Cross, transferred from the Almoraima convent chapel to the new village church in 1972. Mounted pilgrims take part in a colourful procession and there's a flamenco competition.

To reach the main coastal highway, the N340, offering a short run back to Estepona, you can take the CA533 towards Sotogrande or the CA513 to San Martín del Tesorillo and San Roque Torre Guadiaro.

Cork Oak Wilderness

Jimena is a good base for hikes and exploring Los Alcornocales Nature Park. Covering 170,000 hectares, this is said to be the largest Mediterranean park in Europe. Drive up the CA3331, along the Hozgarganta valley. Deer, mongooses, wildcats and birds of prey inhabit the park, a sparsely-inhabited area of rocky outcrops and slopes clad in alcornocales (cork oaks).

Amid the woods, some 24 kilometres from Jimena – in the remotest corner of Málaga province – is La Sauceda, an abandoned settlement converted into a recreational zone with a campsite and 25 spartan stone cabins for rent. For information and reservations, call 902 23 23 30.

The area's inaccessibility always attracted outlaws, rebels and smugglers. Although a chapel, a school and mills were built here in 1923, many inhabitants had no documentation and, in the Civil War, they refused to submit to Franco's forces. The village was bombed, houses were destroyed and the people fled into the hills.

The lonely venta at Puerto de Galis – a little further along the road towards Ubrique and Arcos de la Frontera – was a traditional meeting place for outlaws. Today it serves tasty meals.

Horse amid spring flowers

Village Veteran

1 In the steps of Caesar

WHAT TO SEE

Casares:

Castillo, open daily, entry free.

Casa Natal Blas Infante, Carrera, 51. Museum due to open in 2002.

Gaucín:

Castillo del Aguila. Open Oct-May 10am-1.30pm, 3-6pm, June-Sept 10am-1.30pm, 4-7.30pm, closed Mon.

Museo Etnográfico, Avda Ana Toval. Artefacts from the past. Open Sat, Sun 12-2pm, 4-7pm, summer 7-10pm.

Iglesia de San Sebastián, built 1505 and refurbished in baroque style. Open during mass.

Jimena:

Real Fábrica de Artillería, remains of 18th-century artillery factory.

Santuario Nuestra Señora Reina de Los Angeles, Estación de Jimena. Founded 1450, beautiful cloister, baroque Virgin's quarters.

WHERE TO STAY

Casares:

Casares, Copera, 52. Tel. 952 89 52 11. Former Civil Guard barracks and granary. Fine views. Accessible only on foot. €€

Gaucín:

Casablanca, Calle Teodoro de Molina, 12. Tel. 952 15 10 19. Intimate hotel in tastefully adapted old house. Garden, pool. €€€

La Almuña, Apartado 20, Gaucín (6.2km west of Gaucín off A369). Tel. 952 15 12 00. English-run country-house style cortijo. Pool, tennis, horses. Recommended food. €€€€

Castellar:

La Almoraima, Former convent, antique furniture. Tennis courts, pool. Four-wheel-drive vehicles and horses available for excursions. Local specialities in restaurant. €€€

Jimena:

Anon, Rambling English-run hostal, converted in rustic style from six houses. Consuelo, 30-40. Tel: 956 64 01 13. €€

WHERE TO EAT

Casares:
La Bodeguita de Enmedio, Plaza de España, 15. Tel. 952 89 40 36. Grilled rabbit, lamb.

Gaucín:
La Fructuosa, Luis de Armiñan 67. Tel. 617 692 784, 952 15 10 72. Closed Wed, Thurs, all Nov. Imaginative Mediterranean-inspired dishes in a tastefully converted structure once used for making wine.

Nacional, San Juan de Díos, 8. Tel. 952 15 10 29. Traditional home cooking.

El Pilar, Ctra Algeciras (opposite petrol station). Local dishes. Pool. Terrace with good views.

Jimena:
Hostal Anon restaurant, Consuelo, 30-40. Tel: 956 64 01 13.

Castellar:
La Almoraima restaurant, A369. Tel: 956 69 30 02. Local specialities.

MORE INFORMATION

Casares:
Tourist Office, Ayuntamiento, Calle Fuente, 91. Tel. 952 89 41 26. Open Mon-Fri 9am-2pm.

Gaucín:
Gestur, Lorenzo García, 26. Tel. 952 15 16 00. Open Mon-Fri 10am-1pm, 6-8pm. Specialising in rural accommodation.

Jimena:
Iglesia de la Misericordia. Tel. 956 64 05 69. Open 11am-1pm, 5-7pm daily. Information point for Alcornocales Nature Park.

Outlaw Country

View of Alpandeire

CONTRABAND-RUNNERS, REBELS AND OUTLAWS ONCE ROAMED THE REGION THIS ROUTE TRAVERSES. IT IS ONE OF SOUTHERN SPAIN'S MOST SCENIC ROUTES, CLIMBING MORE THAN 1,000 METRES ABOVE SEA LEVEL THROUGH WILD SIERRAS.

AREA: inland from western Costa del Sol
ROUTE: Estepona→Jubrique→Algatocín→Benadalid→Alpandeire→
Igualeja →San Pedro→Estepona
DISTANCE: 160 kilometres

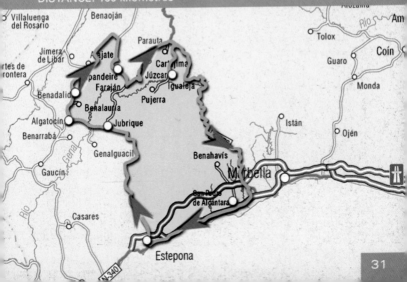

From Estepona you take the MA557, a tortuous, little-travelled road through mountains where anti-Franco guerrillas hid out during the 1940s. After 15 kilometres you reach the Peñas Blancas pass, 1000 metres up on the Sierra Bermeja. A narrow side road leads four kilometres to a barbecue and picnic area and a refuge (not equipped for overnight stays).

Near the refuge and a lookout point with magnificent views of the coast is a bust of Edmond Boissier, who visited in 1837, a scientist credited with informing the world at large of the uniqueness of the *pinsapo* (abies pinsapo Boiss), a Spanish fir found nowhere else in Europe but which flourishes on these slopes. It prefers cold, damp places more than 1000 metres above sea level.

From here you can reach Los Reales, at 1450 metres the summit of this sierra, by a bad road.

North of Peñas Blancas you enter the land of the chestnuts as the MA557 serpentines down steeply to Jubrique and the Genal river. Every year around 4.5 million kilos of chestnuts are harvested in the Genal valley.

Sleepy Jubrique spills down the mountainside. Near its 16th-century San Francisco de Asis church, with an octagonal clock tower, a ceramic plaque notes some local customs and traditions – ask the locals for details of "the legend of the headless priest".

Beyond Jubrique a road branches left to remote Genalguacil ("Gardens of the Vizir" in Arabic). Long neglected, this village has become an immaculate showplace, glowing with flowers and adorned with numerous modern sculptures. Every August, invited artists work in the village, donating their latest creations.

Within Genalguacil's boundaries are traces of ancient gold and silver mines. In the 19th century there were 25 distilleries producing *aguardiente*, until the dreaded phylloxera wiped out the grapevines, which were replaced with chestnuts.

More recently, Genalguacil was the home of El Rubio, an indomitable character who following the Spanish Civil War fought with a guerrilla group against the Franco regime. Believed to have been killed in an ambush, he hid out for 27 years in a farmhouse near the village, finally emerging only in 1976.

From the Genal river, the MA536 climbs to reach the Ronda road at Algatocín. This typical sierra village, whose name has Berber roots, is spectacularly framed by cherry blossom in February. At any time of the year it appears in danger of sliding into the abyss below. El Quejigo, on the highway, sells excellent cured sausage and other local products.

Diverting from our route, if you turn left on the A369 towards Gaucín (see Excursion 1), you reach the breezy Puerto del Espino, well over 600 metres up. Television and telecommunications antennae rise above the road at the crossroads where Venta Solera (menu of the day for around six euros) stands.

A side road plunges northwards down to the Guadiaro valley threaded by the Algeciras-Ronda railway line, while a little further along the A369 another side road takes you to Benarrabá. It straddles a ridge, offering spectacular views, and is a good base for exploring the district, on foot or bike or in four-wheel-drive.

Returning to our route, we continue northeast from Algatocín towards Ronda on the A369, following the ridge between the deep Guadiaro and Genal valleys. Across the valley you glimpse splashes of whitewash, villages clinging to the mountainside amid forests of chestnut, pine, fir and oak trees.

Down to the right lies one of these tiny villages, Benalauría, a labyrinth of alleys and streets little changed over the centuries. It has a good restaurant and also an interesting workshop-museum, La Molienda Verde. Here you can see how chestnuts are prepared for sale - try those conserved in brandy. In a large 18th-century mill, equipment used for crushing olives to extract the oil is on show, along with the various traditional tools employed in local agriculture.

Horse Fair in Ronda

Old customs still hold sway in these villages far from the coastal frenzy. In the first week of August, Benalauría celebrates its annual fair dedicated to Santo Domingo de Gúzman, featuring a piece of theatre based on the struggles between Moors and Christians.

A similar Moors v Christians drama is staged in the next village along the highway, Benadalid, in the third week of August. The village's patron saint is stolen by the Moors and the Christians try to retrieve it. No prizes for guessing who wins every year. Benadalid can claim at least one distinction from its neighbours —its cemetery is located inside the walls of the old Moorish fort.

Occupying an old distillery devoted to producing the mouth-stinging local *aguardiente*, Benadalid's bar-restaurant-museum El Alambique is worth a visit.

Shortly before Atajate (said to be Málaga province's smallest village), the MA508 branches left, corkscrewing down to Jimera de Líbar in the Guadiaro valley. Take this road if you want to visit the Pileta cave (see Excursion 8). Continuing on the A369, the hills are bleak and stony as we climb towards the pass of Encinas Borrachas (Drunken Oaks) and Ronda.

But we can leave Ronda for later as we're heading for some of the least-known villages in these mountains. Holm oaks, junipers, pines and chestnuts clothe abrupt slopes pierced by caves and chasms, providing cover for a wide variety of wild life. A turn to the right takes us along the MA515 to Alpandeire. This village may have only just over 300 inhabitants but its church has been dubbed La Catedral de la Serranía because of its unusual size.

In some gardens you will find a statue of Fray Leopoldo and the main square is called the Plaza Fray Leopoldo. These are tributes to one of Alpandeire's most famous sons. Born in Alpandeire in 1864 of a poor peasant family, Leopoldo received little education but found his vocation at 35 when he joined the Capuchine monks. As he patrolled the streets of Granada collecting alms for the poor, his benign aspect, his white beard and his selflessness eventually made him a legendary figure. By the time he died in 1956, he was regarded as a saint with miraculous powers.

Genalguacil street scene

The village of Algatocín

Ronda and the villages of Alpandeire, Cartajima, Faraján, Igualeja, Júzcar and Parauta are promoting the Route of Fray Leopoldo in a bid to attract more visitors. They are creating information centres, lookout points and better signposting in this rugged terrain, a land of eagles, vultures and wild goats, hidden cascades and somnolent hamlets.

Our route takes us past Faraján, Júzcar (see the 16th-century Santa Catalina church) and Cartajima. Just before reaching the main highway, take a right to visit tiny Parauta. This is the first "ecological village" in the province, its concern for the environment having won it a coveted award. There's an impressive forest of pinsapos nearby.

We turn right on the A376 and then almost immediately branch off to Igualeja. This municipality has two claims to fame: it is where the Río Genal gushes forth from a grotto and it produces fine sausages and other pork products. Take a look at the 16th-century parish church. It shelters sculptures dating back more than 300 years and is guarded by a tower that was once part of a mosque.

Four kilometres beyond Igualeja lies Pujerra, truly the end of the road. It's worth visiting if only for its spectacular situation. An oddity worth looking out for is the Greek lettering to be found on the bricks of some houses. Apparently these came from Christian tombs dating back to 200AD. Pujerra is particularly proud of its large band and the fact that it has a dance of its own, known as the fandangos de Pujerra.

Head back to the A376 to drive back to the coast. To the left rises the massive bulk of the Sierra de las Nieves, protected as a nature park. This 18,550-hectare wilderness area, crossed by few trails, is the home of large stands of the pinsapo as well as deer, otters and golden eagles. Its highest peaks are Enamorados, 1789 metres high, and Torrecillas, 1919 metres.

Built in the 1970s, the A376 makes clever use of the terrain to avoid very steep gradients as it coils downwards to San Pedro de Alcántara on the coast.

WHAT TO SEE
Genalguacil:
Permanent open-air exhibition of modern art.

Benalauría:
Museo Etnográfico, Calle Alta. Tel. 952 15 25 48. Milling equipment in 18th-century olive oil mill. Open Sat, Sun, holidays 1-2pm, 4-6pm. Other days call beforehand.

Benadalid:
El Alambique, Clavero, 6 Bajo. Tel. 952 15 27 71. Bar-restaurant with wine press and old distilling equipment on show.Open Mon-Thurs 12am-4pm, 6.30-11pm, Fri, Sat, Sun 12am-12pm. Closed Wed.

WHERE TO STAY
Benarrabá:
Banu Rabbah, Sierra Bermeja, s/n. Tel. 952 15 02 88. Two-star hotel run by young local cooperative. Fine views. Pool. Excursions possible. €€

Jubrique:
Taha Baja, Algatocín, s/n. Tel. 952 15 23 76. Small family hotel with simple comfortable rooms. Good views. €

Júzcar:
La Posada del Arriero, Tel. 952 18 36 60. Traditional-style decor on site of an ancient inn for muleteers. Simple but comfortable, family-run. Meals. Breakfast included. €€

WHERE TO EAT
Jubrique:
Venta San Juan, Ctra Algatocín-Jubrique, Jubrique. Tel. 952 15 20 55. Shady spot by Río Genal. Grilled lamb, quail, rabbit casserole. Local specialities on sale.

Benalauría:
Mesón La Molienda, Moraleda, 59, Benalauría. Tel. 952 15 25 48. Typical local dishes served in a traditional setting.

Jimera de Líbar:
Quercus, Estación. Tel. 952 18 00 41. Tues-Thurs lunch only. Closed Mon. Agreeable restaurant serving Mediterranean cuisine. Also local dishes.

MORE INFORMATION
Ronda
Tourism office, Paseo de Blas Infante, s/n. Tel. 952 18 71 19. Open Mon-Fri 9.30am-6.30pm, Sat-Sun 10am-2pm, 3.15-6.30.

Sierra de Las Nieves Nature Park information point, Palacio de Mondragón, Ronda. Tel. 952 87 84 50.

Algatocín:
Town Hall, Tel 952 15 00 00

Alpandeire:
Town Hall, Tel. 952 18 02 54

Benadalid:
Town Hall, Tel. 952 15 27 53

Benarrabá:
Town Hall, Tel. 952 15 00 77

Genalguacil:
Town Hall, Tel. 952 15 20 03

Jubrique:
Town Hall, Tel 952 15 22 50

Júzcar:
Town Hall, Tel 952 18 35 00.

Taking the Cure

The mountain village of Tolox

A ROYAL HUNTERS' HIDEAWAY, HEALTH-GIVING WATERS AND WILD COUNTRY WHERE THE LAST OF THE BANDOLEROS ONCE ROAMED. THEY ALL LIE IN THE MOUNTAINS THAT LOOM DRAMATICALLY BEHIND MARBELLA.

AREA: Interior Málaga province
ROUTE: Marbella→Ojén→Monda→Tolox→Alozaina→El Burgo→
Casarabonela→Coin→Fuengirola→Marbella
DISTANCE: 170 kilometres

The modern A355 highway, branching off the Marbella bypass, speeds the journey to the interior. Turn off to visit the village of Ojén (pop. 2000) which at 300 metres above sea-level stands sentinel over the green valley of the Río Real. Dive down into its narrow streets from the main road and take a stroll.

On the Plaza de Andalucía, giant red lilies bloom next to the gushing fountain. On the church wall, a plaque carries an impassioned appeal against "bad and barbarous war". Somebody is always whitewashing. Despite its nearness to the coast, Ojén retains its character.

In archetypal village bars old codgers ponder the past. Dominoes are slapped down. And the prices are a little different from those reigning in tourist haunts just down the road.

Ojén, once famed for its fiery fennel-flavoured anisette, has a wine museum appropriately located in an 18th-century building that once housed a noted distillery. An unusual collection of wine labels, a wide range of information and 120 different wines available for sampling make it a must-visit.

Continuing on the A355, you climb over a pass and shortly after it a left turn takes you six kilometres up a lonely valley to the Refugio de Juanar. This is a comfortable hotel. Once a hunting palace stood here, owned by the wealthy Larios family (Calle Larios in Málaga is named after a Marqués de Larios), who entertained guests such as King Alfonso X111.

Surrounded by trees, the low buildings offer tranquillity in an ideal setting, with plenty of outdoor activities if you are looking for them. Cherry blossom greets spring visitors. One guest was General de Gaulle, who stayed here in 1970 when he was writing his memoirs. On cold days a log fire burns in the lounge, where goat and deer horns hang on the walls. Partridge and roast kid are usually on the Refugio menu.

Hunters come here in season in quest of Spanish ibex, the wild mountain goat, for Juanar lies in the 23,000-hectare Serranía de Ronda hunting reserve. Trails lead off into the Sierra Blanca, to

Istán and Ojén, if you want to do some hiking. Forests of pine, oak, chestnut and eucalypt clothe surrounding slopes and observant walkers may sight anything from wildcats to eagles. Early morning and evening are the best times.

Walk about two kilometres along the bumpy track from the Refugio to reach a lookout point. This is the closest you can get to flying over the Costa del Sol without stepping into an aircraft. Standing 1000 metres above the azure Mediterranean, the lookout point offers a breath-taking view of Marbella and the Mediterranean—and on clear days of the mountains of Africa.

Back on the main road, the scenery grows wilder as you penetrate the sierras, until Monda (pop. 1700) appears, squeezed into a valley. It is an insignificant sort of place, but it does have a (disputed) claim to fame—in the year 40 BC, Roman armies fought a mighty battle near here. Julius Caesar crushed Pompey's forces and went on to conquer the rest of the empire.

On a crag above Monda stands a much-restored castle. The original fortress was pulled down in 1570, after the ill-fated Morisco rising. Arévalo de Zuazo expelled the local inhabitants and handed over all they possessed to eight Christians. A German aristocrat started rebuilding the castle in the early 1970s. Now it is an English-run hotel.

Take the road north to Guaro and the A366, the Málaga-Ronda road. Turn left and, within eight kilometres, before it crosses the Río Grande, a side-road takes you to Tolox (pop. 3500). Tolox's buildings are glued to a steep hillside, each one seeming to balance perilously on the shoulders of the one below it.

Keep left rather than entering the village centre. You pass a riverbed where donkeys and mules are likely to be grazing, then the road, shaded by gums, coils up a delightful valley.

At the end lies a sand-coloured building with a green-tiled roof, the Balneario de Fuente Amargosa (open from mid-June to mid-October), standing above a river tumbling over rocks. This spa's waters pour out at a temperature of 21 degrees Centigrade. Their radioactive qualities are said to be particularly beneficial for those suffering from such ailments as asthma, sinusitis and bronchitis.

Above the Balneario the statue of a wild goat perches on a rock, a reminder that the adjacent Sierra de las Nieves nature park, 18,550 hectares in area, is one of the last refuges of the Capra hispanica.

Eucalypts throw shade over a flat promontory above the murmuring river waters, an ideal spot for a picnic. It is not always so quiet in Tolox. During the San Roque fiesta in mid-August, thousands of rockets are launched when the saint is carried in procession.

Continuing towards Ronda, we pass Alozaina (pop. 3000), a prize-winner for its prettiness but with another attraction. It has one of the few petrol stations around here. Turn into the village to the esplanade where a weekly market is held. The Bar Nuevo offers seats outside in the shade.

The country grows ever wilder as the A366 weaves upwards through pine plantations towards the Sierra de las Nieves. Just after the Jorox pass, pause for breath and admire the panorama. Crags and chasms run into the misty distance, while close at hand several cortijos and terraces of citrus orchards have been squeezed into a cleft.

An old watch tower stands above Yunquera. It has been renovated in strangely gaudy style, pink cement covering the upper part. Climb up over Las Abejas (the bees) Pass at 820 metres. To the left rises the Sierra de las Nieves. This rugged wilderness park, dominated by the 1919-metre Torrecilla peak, is the home of the pinsapo, the rare Spanish fir. To the right soar the rugged slopes of the Sierra Prieta.

It is not surprising that in the past this area was a refuge for outlaws. Around here Pasos Largos (Big Steps), a murderous poacher known as the Last of the Bandoleros, was hunted by the Civil Guard in the 1930s. He was born near the next village, El Burgo.

El Burgo (pop. 2200) sits in an amphitheatre of mountains. Approaching from the eastern flank, you see its church jutting above a hillock thickly clothed with cactus. Remains of an old Roman road and a Moorish castle are to be found here.

For some magnificent views, continue on the A366, the Ronda road, skirting pine forest and rocky buttresses, as far as the Mirador del Guarda Forestal. Park the car and walk up this crag, topped by a limestone statue of a forest guard and a boy. The view down to El Burgo and over the sierras is tremendous, the air like champagne.

In El Burgo ask for the Ardales road, recently improved. You drive through the village and wind through largely unpopulated country. We follow the MA445, which swings right towards Casarabonela, passing below the Prieta peak, 1521 metres high.

There are good picnic spots up here before the road starts descending, offering views across to the fertile Guadalhorce valley. Casarabonela (pop. 2800), a snowdrift of a village, is lodged below woods and sierra. It has remains of a Moorish fortress, plus traces of two Roman roads, to Ronda and to Málaga. A Moorish-style archway gives entrance to the village, where swifts practise aerobatics about the blue-and-white-tiled steeple atop the parish church tower.

On December 12, all the lights of the village are extinguished for one of the province's oldest and most spectacular fiestas. Men bearing flaming torches light the way for the Virgen de los Rondeles as she is borne through the streets to the accompaniment of carol singing.

Orange trees flourish on the well-watered terraces below the village. Following the MA403, we run downhill to the Guadalhorce fertile valley, flowing with the dark green of citrus orchards.

Three kilometres before Pizarra, take a right turn across Arroyo de las Cañas towards Cártama. The white houses of Pizarra are glimpsed across the river (see Excursion 4).

Taking the Cure

The broad road swoops along through irrigated farmland. Side tracks branch off to orange groves. It is easy to get lost on these tracks as there are virtually no signposts. By the wide riverbed of the Río Grande there are shady spots for picnics.

Joining the A355, near Cártama, you can run straight back to Marbella, passing by Coín (pop. 20,000), an agricultural centre making few concessions to tourism. The Moors founded Castro Dazcuan here in 929. Where they prayed to Mecca is now the site of Santa María de la Encarnación church.

Once known as "The town of the 300 orchards", Coín's fertile, well-watered countryside produces large amounts of fruit, particularly oranges and lemons.

Coín–Ronda road

Alternatively, from Cártama a 10-kilometre road cuts across the farmland, known as the Hoya de Málaga, to Alhaurín el Grande.

Three kilometres beyond Alhaurín, on the A387, you reach the Puerto de los Pescadores. The 1150-metre-high Sierra de Mijas soars to the left. Near the crossroads are several eating places and also the four-star Hotel Alhaurín Golf.

You can take a back road to Fuengirola, scything downwards through pleasant rolling country, passing dry hills and scattered farmhouses. Or you turn left and stick with the A387 to Mijas.

View towards El Burgo

Taking the Cure

WHAT TO SEE
Ojén:
Museo del Vino, Carrera, 39. Open 11am-3pm, 4-8pm (summer 6-10pm). Tel. 952 88 14 53. All you need to know about wine, plus different vintages to try. Tourist information. Multilingual staff.

Tolox:
Casa Museo, Plaza Alta. Open 11am-2pm, 4-7pm, closed Mon. Tel. 952 48 73 33. Information office and house furnished in local 19th-century style.

WHERE TO STAY
Ojén:
La Posada del Angel, Mesones, 21. Tel. 952 88 15 88. Intimate Moorish-style hotel, each room with different decor. Village centre. €€€.

Refugio de Juanar, Sierra Blanca. Tel: 952 88 10 00. Former hunting lodge in depths of sierras. Restaurant. €€€

Guaro:
El Molino Santisteban, A366 km 52-53. Tel. 952 45 37 48. Tranquil, six-room Dutch-run hotel. €€

El Burgo:
La Casa Grande, Mesones, 1. Tel. 952 16 02 32. Three stars. Old house restored in traditional style. Restaurant. €€

Casarabonela:
Alcaparaín, Avenida Federico Muñoz, 14. Tel. 952 45 68 43. Two-star hotel, with views over the valley. €

La Era, Los Cerrillos, parcela 85, Casarabonela. Tel. 952 11 25 25/38. Hilltop location. Nine rooms, each decorated in different style. Pool. Meals served. €€€

WHERE TO EAT
Coín:
Venta Río Grande, Ctra Coín-Ronda (A366), km 52, Coín. Tel. 952 45 22 45. Large basic venta.

Yunquera:
El Castillo, Ctra Ronda. Tel. 952 48 04 28. Venta-style. Try the potaje, a rich broth.

El Burgo:
Hotel La Casa Grande. Local specialities.

Alhaurín El Grande:
Venta Los Morenos, Cruce Alhaurín-Mijas-Coín. Tel: 952 49 11 93.
Closed Thurs. Good-value venta fare.

MORE INFORMATION
Tolox:
Tourist office, Casa Museo (see WHAT TO SEE).

Yunquera:
Tourist office, La Venta, 2. Tel. 952 48 26 09.

El Burgo:
Tourist office, Hoyo del Bote, 16. Tel. 952 16 02 41.

Ronda:
Tourist office, Sierra de Las Nieves Nature Park information point,
Palacio de Mondragón. Tel. 952 87 84 50.

Public fountain in Ojén

Málaga's
Lake District

Guadalhorce Lake

SPECTACULAR MOUNTAIN SCENERY, A DELIGHTFUL LAKE-LAND PICNIC SPOT, A ONCE-FASHIONABLE SPA MAKING A COMEBACK AND A COLOURFUL DASH OF HISTORY MAKE THIS A TRIP FOR ALL SEASONS.

AREA: Guadalhorce valley north of Málaga
ROUTE: Málaga→Alora→Chorro→Lakes→Teba →Carratraca→Málaga
DISTANCE: 160 kilometres

From Málaga take the A357, a four-lane highway that whisks you out of the city. It crosses the Río Guadalhorce and a road from Churriana before skirting Cártama and heading northwest towards Carratraca. Sun-bleached, eroded hills border the Guadalhorce valley, green with thousands of citrus and avocado trees.

About 14 kilometres from Cártama, turn right to reach Pizarra, a cluster of white houses below grey and ochre rock faces. Possibly the village's most interesting feature is an unusual municipal museum.

To reach it, drive just over two kilometres south on the MA402 towards Málaga. Housed in the 19th-century Cortijo de Casablanca, the museum shelters 5,000 items collected over 20 years by the New York film director and artist Gino Hollander. Exhibits include Iberian ceramics, Roman glass and antique furniture.

Continue north up the A343. It winds through lonely sierras to Valle de Abdalajís and Antequera, but you swing left over the river and scale the heights to reach Álora (pop. 14,000). The town's massive 17th-century Encarnación church - reputedly the largest in the province after Málaga cathedral - rises amid dwellings cascading down the slopes.

You enjoy fine views from the ochre ramparts of Álora castle. Inside the much-restored walls is a cemetery with a small 15th-century hermitage. Phoenicians and Romans followed by Visigoths and Moors fortified these strategic heights. It is advisable to park in Plaza Baja, immediately below the castle.

On the outskirts of the town, veer right towards El Chorro. From here on the driving gets serious as the road narrows and twists and turns. The abundant water encourages the cultivation of a variety of crops and tropical fruit.

Then the mountains close in until we are passing through a steep-sided chasm, the river Guadalhorce tumbling along below us. Watch for sudden dips in the road.

A solid barrier of rock looms ahead, apparently blocking the valley. Here you find one of the most spectacular sights in Andalusia. The Guadalhorce river flows through the Garganta del Chorro. It looks as though a knife has sliced through the rock to create this deep gorge.

Turn right over the dam below El Chorro. The road winds up to a station on the Málaga-Córdoba line. Before it reaches the station a track goes off to the left.

Follow this if you are in adventurous mood. A footpath winds along the hillside to reach the rail track. You pass across the railway bridge to gain access to the Camino del Rey (the King's Path). King Alfonso X111 is supposed to have taken a walk along here in 1921 when he opened the Guadalhorce dams.

He could not have suffered from vertigo. The catwalk clings like a fly to the rock face and vaults the gorge by way of a bridge. There are plans to repair the catwalk but at the moment it is in a dangerously bad state and you should not attempt to walk along it.

Near the station are a bar and restaurant and several places offering accommodation. There are good hiking and climbing possibilities in the area. If you follow the paved road beyond the station over the hills, you reach Valle de Abdalajís. But we're heading north towards the lakes. From El Chorro the narrow road, edges crumbling, climbs past pines and eroded rock.

Shortly after passing a shrine in honour of the Virgin of Villaverde, patron of Ardales, and the Bar La Ermita, you take a left turn into ancient history. A six-kilometre road soars up to a flat-topped mountain where 1000 years ago Bobastro - capital of a rebel kingdom - was located.

Omar Ben Hafsun is said to have used this as his base in his wars with the Caliph of Córdoba. You can see why. It is virtually impregnable. Remains of old walls can be found, as well as caves inhabited in Moorish times. A modern curiosity is the large reservoir that occupies part of the summit; its waters tumble down the mountain to generate power for Málaga.

Look for a sign indicating the Mozarab church. A walk of a few hundred yards from the road takes you to this unique structure hewn from the rock. The foundations of a second Mozarab church, dating back to the ninth century, were discovered nearby in 2001.

Back on the main road, continue to a T-junction. Ahead lie the emerald waters of Lago Turón, one of the three Guadalhorce lakes that provide water for Málaga province.

Turn right on MA444 to wind along through pine forests with the lake glinting on your left. Soon you encounter an information office for the Parque Ardales, a campsite and picnic tables. You can hire canoes here. Anglers fish for carp, black bass and pike.

El Mirador Restaurant is an ideal spot to enjoy lunch in the shade as the breeze sings through the pines. The road runs through a tunnel under the restaurant. A little further along is another good-value restaurant, El Kiosko, with views over the dam.

Continue along the lakeside road until you cross a dam. Turn right to explore further the lake area and hydraulic works. Two hundred metres along on the right you come to a hotel and the restaurant El Oasis.

Return over the dam and head towards Ardales (pop. 3000), a typical sierra village of interlocking houses, topped by the usual Arab fortress. Well worth viewing is the well-organised museum. The Mudéjar parish church dates from the 15th century. On the west of Ardales, a Roman bridge, Puente de la Molina, is still in use. A dusty track beyond leads to the 13th-century Nazari fort of Turón.

For an unusual story of Scottish heroism, make a 15-kilometre detour to the north, to Teba (pop. 4500), straddling a rocky outcrop crowned by the ruins of La Estrella castle.

Pause in the town at the Plaza de España. A monument of white Scottish granite commemorates the heroism of a warrior who fell in battle here in 1330. Following a deathbed request from Scotland's King Robert the Bruce, Sir James Douglas—known because of his dark complexion as the Black Douglas—agreed to take Robert's heart to the Holy Land. En route, he became entangled with King Alfonso X1 of Castile's wars with the Moors.

In the siege of Teba, he was surrounded and, after defiantly hurling the casket containing the royal heart at the Moorish horsemen, he was cut down. Lord Selkirk, representing the Douglas clan, unveiled the memorial in 1989.

Pig-breeding and leather manufacture are modern sources of income in Teba and neighbouring Campillos. On the Campillos-Antequera highway you will find several large showrooms offering leatherware.

Retracing our steps to Ardales, we head south on the Alora road, passing by the Cueva de Ardales. Also known as the Doña Trinidad Cave after a well-known 19th-century Málaga personality, this has spectacular stalactites, 20,000-year-old paintings and traces of Neolithic man. The number of visitors is tightly controlled and there is a two-month waiting list in summer.

A short drive through the olive and almond trees brings us to "the Diamond of Málaga", Carratraca, a spa which in its heyday last century attracted everybody from Lord Byron to Alexandre Dumas. The mineral-rich waters of the stone-built balneario are beneficial for skin troubles, nervous diseases and a variety of other complaints.

When the beautiful Empress Marie Eugenie, wife of Napoleon 111 and Countess of Teba, visited, three gambling casinos were flourishing in Carratraca. In 1830 King Fernando V11 even ordered an inn, El Príncipe, built for himself and his courtiers. This creaky, rambling establishment is being refurbished and expanded and plans include a five-star hotel and a costly facelift for the baths. Carratraca could once again become a fashionable spot.

If you are in the area during Easter Week, do not miss El Paso, the Carratraca passion play, enacted by more than 100 villagers—one-seventh of the population—in the bullring on Good Friday and Easter Saturday. Remarkably, this popular event owes its origins to a Canadian, Vancouver-born James Blaine Rutledge, who dusted off an old text and organised the first Paso in 1975.

From Carratraca, route MA 441 rocks and rolls around the dry hills to Álora. But a more comfortable, direct ride back is offered by the new road, the A357, that runs down to Málaga.

Paragliding outside of Teba Castle

El Chorro

WHAT TO SEE

Álora:
Álora Castle. Open 10am-1pm, 4.30-6pm. Fine views, Mudéjar arch.

Encarnación church, 17th century;

Pizarra:
Museo Municipal, Cortijo Casa Blanca, Ctra Cártama-Álora 2.3 km from Pizarra. Tel. 952 48 32 37. Open 10am-2pm, 4-8pm, closed Mon.

Ardales:
Museo de la Historia y las Tradiciones, open 10.30am-2pm, 5-7pm, closed Mon.

Cueva de Ardales, open April-September, call 952 45 80 46/87 to arrange guided visits, limited to 15 persons daily. Paleolithic drawings.

Teba:
Museo Histórico, Plaza de la Constitución. Open Sat-Sun 12-2pm, 6.30-8.30pm, weekdays by prior arrangement (tel. 952 74 80 20).

Archeological finds, especially Roman.

WHERE TO STAY

El Chorro:
La Garganta, Apartments in a renovated mill. Pool, climbing wall, restaurant. €€€

Ardales:
La Posada del Conde, Pantano del Chorro, 16, Ardales. Tel. 952 11 24 11. Three stars. Sauna. Beautifully located by the lakes. €€€

Cortijo Valverde, Crta de Álora/Valle de Abdalajís, km 35.5, Alora. Tel. 952 11 29 79. Seven rooms at an off-the-beaten-track, converted farmhouse. Pool. English spoken. €€€

WHERE TO EAT

Ardales:

Restaurante El Oasis, Pantano del Chorro, Ardales. Tel: 95-245 81 02. Excellent roast lamb and rabbit. Can be crowded on weekends.

El Mirador and *El Kiosko*, both restaurants overlooking Guadlahorce lakes and offering good value.

El Chorro:

La Garganta restaurant. Tel. 952 49 51 19.

Carratraca:

Venta El Trillo, Ctra Alora-Ardales, km 16. Tel. 952 45 81 99. Friendly welcome at a basic venta.

MORE INFORMATION

Álora:

Tourist office, Avda de la Constitución, 1. Tel. 952 49 83 80. Open: Mon-Fri 10am-2.30pm.

Ardales:

Tourist office, Museo de la Historia y las Tradiciones. Tel. 952 45 80 46. Open 10.30am-2pm, 5-7pm, closed Mon.

Carratraca:

Tourist office, Ayuntamiento, Glorieta, 2. Tel. 952 45 80 16. Tourist office open mornings.

Flamingos and Rock Fantasies

Rock formations near Torcal

A MAGICAL, STRANGELY DISTORTED LANDSCAPE, ONE OF
ANTIQUITY'S GREAT MYSTERIES AND EUROPE'S SECOND
LARGEST COLONY OF FLAMINGOS AWAIT YOU NORTH
OF MÁLAGA.

AREA: north of Málaga
ROUTE: Málaga→Almogía →Villanueva →Torcal→
Antequera→Archidona →Casabermeja→Málaga
DISTANCE: 110 kilometres

Drive up the Avenida de Carlos Haya, northwest from the city centre, towards Puerto de la Torre and Almogía, along C3310, also numbered at this point MA 423.

The area around Puerto de la Torre is popular as a weekend luncheon spot, witness the many ventas along the route. Soon you leave the city bustle and run up a valley where algarrobo trees, cactus, almond and olive trees clothe the slopes.

The MA423 swings over a bridge across the Campanillas River and then twists upwards, offering magnificent views over the countryside. By forking right before the bridge you can take an alternative route north past the Campanillas dam and reservoir, if construction work is not in progress.

Twenty-six kilometres from Málaga, the village of Almogía (pop. 4100) appears on your left, a Moorish tower standing above the houses tumbled over a ridge. Squeeze down the narrow streets to the main square dominated by the *Ayuntamiento* (town hall). Parking is not easy, but the Bar Central on the square is handy if you need refreshment.

A number of foreigners have fled the coast to live in or near tranquil Almogía, but it figures in few guidebooks, even though it claims to be the Cuña de Verdiales (cradle of the ancient, driving singing style of the Montes de Málaga).

A stroll through the streets will give you glimpses of pensioners dozing in doorways, housewives whitewashing. Look for Calle Winters (Almogía is twinned with the town of Winters, near Sacramento, California). For the best views, trek up the concreted track to the ruined tower, topped by a television antenna.

The road, now MA 424, winds through sparsely populated country that finally opens out into an undulating landscape of cornfields, emerald green in spring. In the distance, above the white outline of Villanueva de la Concepción tower the formidable ramparts of El Torcal.

This limestone barrier rose from the sea bed some 150 million years ago. Wind and water have carved the 1200-hectare area into all manner of bizarre shapes. It is possible to envisage the rocks as turrets, reptiles, or animal forms, particularly at twilight.

Past Villanueva the road, once more the C3310, twists upwards towards Antequera. After six kilometres a side turning takes you through tortured rock formations to El Torcal's interpretation centre. An exhibition gives details about the geology and flora and fauna of this nature park, which is controlled by the Junta de Andalucía. There are toilets too!

From a mirador you can enjoy beautiful views over the mountains towards the blue-hazed coast. Follow the Ruta Verde, a marked path, through the labyrinth for a 1.8km walk of one hour. You may well see wild goats lazing on the rocks. Don't stray from the path, to avoid damage to the environment but also because, especially at dusk or in mist, it is easy to get lost and you could spend an uncomfortable night in the open.

You can cut short your trip by returning to Villanueva. From there a good road, the MA436, runs 16 kilometres past fields and almond orchards to Casabermeja, on the main Málaga-Antequera highway.

Alternatively, continue north on the C3310 for 15 kilometres through the Boca del Asno pass to Antequera. There are several ventas on this scenic route. Entering Antequera, you have a fine view of the town's rooftops and Moorish castle and, beyond, an unusual-looking outcrop known as the Peña de los Enamorados.

This peak appears to offer the profile of a human face, gazing up at the heavens. Legend has it that a Moorish damsel fled to the summit with her Christian lover when their families opposed their union. At the top, they embraced and then plunged together to their deaths.

Commanding a fertile plain where everything from sunflowers to asparagus flourish, Antequera (pop. 39,000) has been an important crossroads since ancient times. The Romans established the settlement of Antikaria here and the fortress was a stronghold of the Moorish Kingdom of Granada, falling to the Christian forces in 1410.

Antequera's busy main street is named after Infante Don Fernando, who paved the way for Castile's ousting of the Moors by crushing their army in a battle at a neighbouring chasm, known as the Ass's Mouth.

If you climb up to the Moorish fortress, you pass through an impressive 400-year-old gate, the Arco de los Gigantes. Beyond lies a national monument, the 16th-century Colegiata de Santa María la Mayor, with a Renaissance facade and interior. Addicts of religious architecture have plenty of scope in Antequera, for the town claims to have more churches and convents – at least 30 – than any other Spanish town.

Pride of place in the municipal museum is taken by Efebo, a delightful bronze statue of a boy, dating from the first century AD of the Roman era. Unearthed at a local farm, it has virtually become the town's symbol.

Roman settlement left many traces around Antequera and evidence of earlier civilisations is still coming to light. Whatever you do, don't miss Antequera's greatest mystery, the dolmens. There are three of these well-preserved burial sites, constructed around 4000 years ago by a people of whom we know very little.

The Cueva de Menga, with the Cueva de Viera nearby, is on the edge of town, near the petrol station on the Granada road. See if you can figure out how the megaliths - massive stone slabs, the heaviest weighing 180 tons - were transported here, apparently from the Cerro de la Cruz, one kilometre away.

The Romeral dolmen, further out of town, dates from 1800 BC. Unlike the other dolmens, it is circular with a slate cupula. Objects of value entombed with the dead were found under the slab lodged in the wall of a smaller inner chamber.

While in Antequera you should try a *mollete*, a distinctive type of bread roll baked in a wood oven, and *porra antequerana*, a delicious thick, gazpacho-style cold soup.

Continue east on the A92 to visit the pleasant town of Archidona, Roman name Arcia Domina (Lady of the Heights). Particularly worth visiting is the beautiful Plaza Ochavada, an eight-sided 18th-century square, once the scene of bullfights and markets, now the scene of concerts and other entertainment.

Overlooking the town are the old Moorish fort and the Virgen de la Gracia hermitage, in which you can see the columns of the mosque that once stood here.

Dog-lovers should note that Archidona holds a big Feria del Perro on the first weekend in June. As many as 4000 animals, from hunting dogs to police sniffer dogs, arrive from all over Spain to take part in shows and competitions.

The fastest way back to Málaga from Archidona is via the A92 towards Antequera then the N331. Alternatively, you can wander along country roads by heading south on the MA222 to Villanueva del Trabuco, then the MA224 to Villanueva del Rosario before hitting the auto-route.

The N331 skirts Casabermeja (pop. 3000), a tumble of hillside houses. This village, founded by Queen Isabel's decree in the 16th century, gained brief notoriety in 1840 when farmers ran the biggest landowners out of town and declared the place a republic. Forty horsemen and 40 infantry sent to crush the rising were repelled. Alas, a full-scale army soon put paid to the republic.

The parish church stands at the foot of the main street, Calle Real, which climbs straight to heaven. Downhill, the street reaches the gates of Casabermeja's pride, the cemetery. It is distinguished by some elaborate Moorish style cupolas and rows of tiled tombs. Immediately below, traffic thunders along the highway, 25 kilometres and a few minutes away from Málaga.

Flamingo paradise

Worth a detour, especially in springtime, is the Laguna de Fuente de Piedra, 20 kilometres northwest of Antequera, off the A92. Turn into Fuente and take the road towards Sierra de Yeguas. Head for the Centro de Visitantes where an exhibition explains the special characteristics of the saline lake and its flora and fauna. You can rent binoculars here, essential for a close-up view of the most flamboyant residents: flamingos.

In spring and early summer thousands of these graceful birds nest here. Covering 1300 hectares in rainy years, the lake and the Camargue in France are Europe's most important breeding areas for flamingos. You can drive around the lagoon, stopping at various points to view them and many other bird species.

If you wonder why so many flamingos come here, it is because food is plentiful, particularly tasty molluscs that thrive in the salty waters.

On the road to Torcal

Fuente de Piedra

Easter procession in Archidona's Plaza Ochavada

WHAT TO SEE

Archidona:
Plaza Ochavada, octagonal square in centre of town.

Virgen de la Gracia hermitage. Open 10am-2pm, 4-8pm.

Santa Ana church, Gothic, many art treasures.

Laguna de Fuente de Piedra:
Centro de Visitantes (Tel. 952 11 17 15) open Wed-Sun 10am-2pm, 4-6pm (April-Sept 6-8pm).

Antequera:
Dolmens – Menga and Viera, Ctra N331, 1km from town centre, and *Romeral*, Cerro Romeral, off N331, left at junction of Archidona and Málaga roads. Open Tues 9am-3.30pm, Wed-Sat 9am-6pm, Sun 9.30am-2.30pm, Closed Mon.

Municipal Museum, Palacio de Nájera, Plaza Coso Viejo. Paintings, sculptures. Open Tues-Fri 10am-1.30pm, 4-6pm, Sat 10am-1.30pm, Sun 11am-1.30pm. Closed Mon. Entry 2 euros.

Colegiata de Santa María, Renaissance monument open Tues-Fri 10.30am-2pm, 4.30-6.30pm, Sat 10.30am-2pm, Sun 11.30-2pm. Closed Mon.

Alcazaba - castle, old walls, excellent views.

Iglesia de Los Remedios, 17th-century national monument open 8pm daily. Belén convent - Baroque church. Cakes on sale by the nuns. Open 8am-5.30pm.

WHERE TO STAY

Antequera:
Parador, Paseo García del Olmo, s/n. Tel: 952 84 02 61. Modern building in tranquil spot amid gardens. €€€

Papabellotas, Calle Encarnación, 5. Tel. 952 70 50 45. Centrally located, small modern, well-equipped hotel. Bar, restaurant. €

Archidona:
Santo Domingo, Calle Santo Domingo. Tel. 952 71 70 55. Hotel school in refurbished 16th-century convent, stylish appointed. Opened 2002. Pool, restaurant. €€€

Villanueva de la Concepción: La Posada del Torcal, Ctra La Hoya-La Higuera. Tel. 952 03 11 77. Luxury rustic-style. Closed Nov-Jan. €€€€.

WHERE TO EAT

Antequera:

Plaza de Toros, Paseo María Cristina. Tel. 952 84 46 62. Under the bullring. Imaginative local cuisine. Aubergine with ham and molasses, ox-tail.

El Escribano, Plaza de los Escribanos, 11. Tel. 952 70 65 33. Outdoor dining on esplanade next to Santa María church and Alcázar. Local dishes, including porra antequerana.

Archidona:

Bar Central, Calle Nueva, 49, and Bar La Veleta de las Monjas, Calle Nueva, 44, offer excellent local dishes at good prices.

Hotel Santo Domingo, restaurant with local dishes.

MORE INFORMATION

Antequera:

Tourist office, Plaza de San Sebastián, 7. Tel. 952 70 25 05. Open Mon-Sat 9.30am-1.30pm, 4-7pm, Sun 10am-2pm.

Archidona:

Tourist office, Plaza Ochavada, 2. Tel. 952 71 64 79. Open Tues-Fri 10am-2pm, Tues & Thurs 4-6pm, Sat & Sun 11am-2pm.

Parque Natural El Torcal.

Visitors' Centre. Tel. 952 03 13 89. Open daily 10am-5pm.

Reserva Natural Laguna Fuente de Piedra. Visitors' Centre. Tel. 952 11 17 15. Open Wed-Sun 10am-2pm, 4-6pm (April-Sept 6-8pm).

To Little Madrid and Beyond

Almond blossoms near Comares

EAST OF MÁLAGA LIES A SPECTACULAR AREA OF MOUNTAINOUS COUNTRY SPRINKLED WITH ANCIENT, SUNBLEACHED VILLAGES WHERE 21ST-CENTURY HUSTLE STILL SEEMS A LONG WAY AWAY. THIS WEDGE OF MÁLAGA PROVINCE IS KNOWN AS THE AXARQUIA.

AREA: Axarquía, eastern Málaga province
ROUTE: Málaga→Macharaviaya→Benamocarra→Almáchar →El Borge→Cútar →Comares→Málaga
DISTANCE: 140 kilometres

The coastal resorts of Nerja, Torrox and Torre del Mar attract thousands of visitors. But it's a different story inland.

First stop is a village once so famed for its progress and prosperity that it was dubbed Little Madrid. To reach it, you take the N340 auto-route from Málaga. Shortly after bypassing Rincón de la Victoria, a turnoff near the Añoreta golf course leads along the MA106 to Macharaviaya.

Very soon you are back in Old Spain. The narrow road climbs and twists past olive and almond trees. You begin to descend and sight two villages. To the left is Benaque, where Salvador Rueda, an acclaimed poet, was born in 1857—his house is preserved. To the right, tucked into a fold, is Macharaviaya, its parish church towering over the humble village dwellings.

Traffic is sparse in the main street. Take a good look at that church, a colossal Neo-classical building with a 20-metre nave. Four pillars adorn the main entrance, above which is a coat of arms topped by a crown. Why such an imposing structure in such a small village? The pantheon below the church offers an explanation. To visit it and the church, ask for the key from Amparo who lives at a corner house opposite the church.

The pantheon contains the remains of the Gálvez family, who two centuries ago transformed Marchariaviaya. Soldiers, diplomats, adventurers, they became the favourites of King Carlos 111 and enforced his will in the New World.

In the gloomy vault, with its six alabaster sculptures, look for the grey marble tomb of José de Gálvez, the most prominent of four brothers. His ashes are contained in a large urn.

José rose to become Marquis of Sonora and Minister of the Indies. He played a big part in expelling the Jesuits from Spain's American colonies and moved swiftly to block the Russians moving into California.

His nephew Bernardo fought the Apache Indians, became governor of Louisiana and defied the British in the American War of Independence. Galveston is named after Bernardo and a United States order known as Los Granaderos de Galves still pays tribute to him for his help in beating the Redcoats.

The Gálvez family did not forget their birthplace. They rebuilt the church and packed it with treasures, including (it is said) six Murillo paintings. You will not find any of them there now, as the building was sacked during the Spanish Civil War.

A factory employing 200 people was established to manufacture playing cards and it enjoyed the monopoly of their export to the New World. Traffic bustled along the new carriage route from the coast to the prosperous community with its fine paved streets and bubbling fountains.

Little Madrid's heyday ended with the passing of the illustrious Gálvez family and it sank back into obscurity. But its links with the United States can be read in the street names, Pensacola, Mobile, New Orleans. It is twinned with Mobile.

Refugees from city life have refurbished some of the houses. Potters and painters have moved into Machariaviaya, so close to the United States, so far in temperament from the Costa.

It is possible to take dirt tracks to reach the next stop, Iznate, but these are only for the steely-nerved as they are narrow, sometimes bumpy, and soar along lofty ridges. Ask for directions at the Ayuntamiento.

Safer and simpler to return to the N340, continue east, then take the MA176 to Cajiz and Iznate. There are splendid panoramic views across the hills and valleys to the stark limestone buttress of the Sierra Tejeda. Iznate is an unpretentious village with the 16th-century San Gregorio V11 church its most imposing building.

Less pleasant on the eye are prison-like blocks rising on a neighbouring ridge, the inmates being thousands of pigs. Intensive agriculture holds sway as you approach Benamocarra. Turn left in the centre towards Vélez-Málaga, then quickly left again towards El Borge.

Fields of artichokes and strawberries fill the well-watered river valley, forests of avocado trees clothe the slopes.

Take a left to explore Almáchar. The white cubist houses spill down a cleft in the hills. Eating places are few, but up near the Civil Guard quarters, school premises have been converted into a hotel and a friendly restaurant offering local dishes.

This village has a somewhat unlikely claim to fame as "Capital of the Moscatel Grape and Garlic Soup". The first Saturday in September the decorated streets are thronged with visitors when it holds a fiesta in honour of *ajoblanco*, a delicious cold soup made from garlic and almonds. Flamenco dancing goes on until the early hours as everybody samples the *ajoblanco* and local wine.

From Almáchar the MA149 dips down to the coast, passing by Moclinejo and Benagalbón. However, we head for the interior. After a few bends, El Borge swings into view on the left. Reflecting local sympathies, one street is named after Che Guevara. After the euro arrived in 2002, another street was called Calle de las Pesetas.

A blue-and-white-tiled steeple crowns the octagonal tower of the old church, Nuestra Señora del Rosario, rising above the tumble of dwellings. The tower's Moorish-style brickwork is a reminder of the times when a mosque stood here. Immense pillars support the three naves, one of which shelters an image of El Borge's patron saint, Gabriel.

On the church wall an inscription indicates that a worn stone was for many years used for sharpening spinning tops. More interesting is the church weather vane. If you look hard enough, you may see the hole left by El Bizco when he was demonstrating his marksmanship.

This notorious, one-eyed, 19th-century outlaw was born here. The village is opening a hotel-museum dedicated to the *bandolero* (bandit). Sadly, El Bizco was hardly a figure of romance. In fact, by all accounts, he was a swaggering cut-throat who sowed fear wherever he went.

A handy place to debate this question is the friendly Bar Pepe, in the square next to the church. Pepe and María sell the excellent local moscatel wine, including a lighter version known as Dama de la Virgen.

Every September El Borge stages a Día de la Pasa, when homage to the delicious local raisins is paid in appropriate fashion. Raisins are handed out and the local wine flows freely amid flamenco dancing, singing of verdiales and sampling of typical local dishes.

Continuing inland, we run over a pass and curve downwards. Across a deep valley planted with olive and almond trees and vines a snowdrift crowns the mountain top. That is Comares, known as the Balcony of the Axarquía.

But first we have to descend, past the village of Cútar—"Fuente del Paraíso" as it dubs itself. The big sight is the Aina Alcaharía spring, on the lower road into town. Old mill stones and brickwork decorate this spot where a plaque shows a donkey and the message "Alleviate my thirst as I lighten your work!"

Walk up a few steps to a grill covering a hole in the rock. Mysteriously, a current of warm air emerges.

Hitting the valley bottom where thousands of ripening lemons hang like yellow lanterns amid thick foliage, we reach Benamargosa, a workaday village enjoying something of a boom. Turn left towards Riogordo and Colmenar and, shortly after Salto del Negro, look for the road to Comares on the left. It corkscrews seven kilometres up the mountainside, finally emerging on the summit at 739 metres above sea level.

A lookout point has been constructed off the Comares main plaza. From here you can enjoy a magnificent panorama of bleak mountains, ridges dotted with whitewashed farmhouses, fertile valleys, the growing sprawl of Vélez-Málaga and the Mediterranean coast. Locals claim 12 other villages are visible from Comares.

Verdiales fiesta

The narrow streets were repaved in the 1990s but tread this labyrinth and you can easily imagine you are back in Moorish times. You will encounter archways and alcoves, the 16th-century Encarnación church with its stumpy tower and the cemetery with tombs five decks high. Near the cemetery are the two remaining towers of the Moorish fortress. Comares is noted for its particular style of verdiales, the wild, raucous music native to the Montes de Málaga, and this is commemorated in the Plaza de los Verdiales.

By tradition (it depends on the parish priest), on Sundays and holidays the church bell used to be tolled 30 times. This dates from the Reconquest, when 30 Moslem families converted to Christianity and were baptised in the street known as the Calle del Perdón.

Three kilometres down the Málaga road from the village you can visit ruins of an ancient Moorish settlement. Just before the bar-restaurant El Molino at the Barriada de los Ventorros, a sign on the right indicates the two-kilometre walk up the hillside to Mazmúllar.

Hunt around and you will encounter a hole in the hillside leading to a gallery of intersecting passages, forming nine compartments with domed ceilings. The complex was apparently built by the Moors to store water. Tumbled stones in this area mark the remains of houses inhabited 1000 years ago.

Comares eating places include La Plaza in the main square. Alongside is the Molino de los Abuelos restaurant in a delightful old mill but not always open on weekdays. On the Málaga road are recommended hotel-restaurants the Atalaya and El Molino. Next door to the Molino is an interesting English-run craft shop, El Duende.

For real back roads driving, follow a sign pointing to Colmenar on the MA165 about two kilometres from Comares. The road plunges into a deep valley, crosses a dam, turns to dirt then climbs past renovated farmhouses amid almond trees. After five kilometres you turn left at a T-junction and continue over lofty ridges seven kilometres to Colmenar and the Málaga highway.

Prefer the easy way home? Stick to the MA165 that swoops over the crests of the hills from Comares to reach the old Málaga-Granada road, the C345.

Cútar with Comares in Background

WHAT TO SEE

Almáchar:
San Mateo church, Mudéjar-style tower.

Museo de la Pasa, Plaza Santo Cristo, 5. Covers cultivation of vines and production of Moscatel raisins, rustic furnishings preserved on first floor, open weekday mornings. Ask at town hall, weekends ask for Pepa who lives nearby.

El Borge:
Rosario church, Moorish-style brickwork. Ask Antonio in adjacent grocery shop for the key; Museo del Bandolero (in preparation).

Parque Ornitológico La Alcua, bird park, open daily; Museo del Sarmiento (Calle Río, 3), traditional farm and domestic tools (call 952 51 21 33 to arrange visit).

Comares:
Moorish arches, towers; panoramic views.

Mazmüllar ruins.

Macharaviaya:
Parish church and Gálvez pantheon, Gálvez Museum. Inquire at town hall about opening hours.

Benaque 16th-century church.

WHERE TO STAY

Almáchar:
Punto Europa, Calle Cornellá de Llobregat, 25. Tel 952 51 95 19. Tiles, brick and woodwork create a welcoming air in the five apartments, with TV and kitchen. Small pool, barbecue. €€€

Comares:
El Molino, Barriada de Los Ventorros, 29. Tel: 952 03 00 12. Converted from an old olive mill. Three double rooms and an apartment. €

Atalaya, Encinillas, s/n. Tel. 952 50 92 08. Located outside the village with fine views. Seven rooms. €€

Moclinejo:
Axarquía, Ctra Moclinejo, km 1. Tel 952 40 05 07. New 12-room,

ochre-walled hotel. Magnificent views. Pleasant rooms, earthenware tiles, beams and brickwork. Large restaurant. €

Near Macharaviaya:
Molino de Santillán, Ctra de Macharaviaya, km3. Tel 952 40 09 49. Closed early Jan-March 1. Stylish living in secluded, converted farmhouse. Gardens, pool. €€€€

WHERE TO EAT

Almáchar:
Mesón Punto Europa (see Where to stay). Next to the Civil Guard quarters, former school dining hall converted into pleasant, wood-beamed bar-restaurant. Ajoblanco, stewed kid and home-made desserts. Good value menu.

El Borge:
Bar Pepe, Plaza de la Constitución. Tel. 952 51 22 37. Friendly village bar. Tapas and local dishes such as baby goat and tripe and chick peas.

Comares:
El Molino (see Where to stay). Rustic venta-style. Blazing fire in winter. Dishes in local style. The lamb chops are recommended.

Macharaviaya:
Taberna El Candil. Serving tapas and hearty low-priced menu of the day.

MORE INFORMATION

Almáchar:
Town Hall, 952 51 20 02.

Comares:
Town Hall, 952 50 92 33.

El Borge:
Town Hall, 952 51 20 33.

Macharaviaya:
Town Hall, 952 40 00 42.

Route of the Wine

Los Pastores: Carol singers in Frigiliana

IMPECCABLE, WHITEWASHED VILLAGES, VINE-AND-OLIVE-CLAD HILLS AND MOUNTAINS THAT REALLY DO LOOK LIKE THE EDGE OF A SAW (SIERRA) MAKE ANY VISIT TO THE AXARQUÍA WORTHWHILE.

AREA: Axarquía (eastern Málaga province)
ROUTE: Nerja→Frigiliana→Torrox→Cómpeta→Sedella→Canillas→
Vélez Málaga→Nerja
DISTANCE: 95 kilometres

From Nerja, head for the hills. The MA105 runs directly inland, crossing a new four-lane *autovía* from Málaga and running past fields of sweet potatoes and avocado orchards towards the sharp-toothed mountains of the Sierra Almijara, declared a protected nature park.

Until recently, Frigiliana (pop. 2100), six kilometres from the coast and 300 metres above sea level, retained the character of a typical agricultural village. Despite what many guidebooks tell you, it was never "voted the most beautiful village" in Spain and Andalusia. Instead, with its cubist architecture and mosaic-cobbled streets, some years back it won prizes as the "best-preserved and beautified" village.

Considerable credit for that goes to a far-sighted mayor who ruled that all building must be low-rise and in traditional Andalusian style. Sadly, today's short- sighted authorities have been far less stringent, allowing a blizzard of inappropriate construction. If you can find a parking spot, the old section of town is still worth a stroll but you may have to elbow your way through busloads of sightseers.

All that remains of the Moorish fort on the hill above the village are traces of old walls, for it was razed 400 years ago after a major battle in the War of Granada. Moriscos (Moors converted to Christianity) made their last stand here against Philip 11's forces but were finally crushed. One of the Frigiliana streets is named after Hernando El Darra, the Morisco leader.

Twelve ceramic plaques dotted about the village recount the epic tale. One reports that the Ajarquía was populated by "slight, strong men of such great spirit that in the old days the Moorish kings regarded them as the most valiant, daring and effective in the Kingdom of Granada".

The local wine, honey and virgin olive oil are available. Molasses is still canned in the Ingenio, the large building near the Civil Guard barracks, the last such factory in Europe.

Beyond the village a paved road curves up the mountainside to Torrox, 14 kilometres away. You pass several ventas offering meals and fine views.

On your right at first is the mass of El Fuerte, a 981-metre-high mountain covered with scrub, esparto grass and gnarled trees, where the Moriscos converts took refuge from Philip 11's forces during their 1569 rebellion.

Men and women hurled rocks down on the advancing soldiers from these heights. Look for a cliff of reddish bare rock. Here, it is said, many Moriscos leaped to their deaths rather than be captured.

The Frigiliana-Torrox road is an unforgettable scenic drive - particularly in February and early March when the almond blossom is out - as the road swoops along ridge crests. The steep hillsides are clothed in vineyards and olive trees and avocadoes, mangoes and custard apples flourish on irrigated terraces.

Think twice before using the road at night. Sharp curves and steep drops are common, crash barriers few. The road loops over a ridge to reveal the town of Torrox, straggling over a ridge.

After crossing a narrow river bridge, be careful not to veer left into Torrox itself. Drivers have been lost for days as they struggled to squeeze through the narrow streets. Instead keep right on the road around the top of the town until you meet the bypass. Turn right towards Cómpeta.

"The Very Noble and Very Loyal Town of Torrox", important as an agricultural centre (pop. 10,000), is said to have been the birthplace of the great Moorish leader, Al-Mansur. An 18th-century parish church stands above a pleasant square with pavement cafes.

On the Sunday before Christmas, Torrox celebrates its Día de las Migas, when thousands arrive to eat *migas* (a leaden concoction of flour or bread crumbs fried in olive oil), drink the powerful local wine, and enjoy fandangos, verdiales and other folk music.

Outside many cortijos on the winding Cómpeta road you will see earth-covered beds, always facing the sun. These are where every autumn moscatel grapes are laid out to dry to prepare some of the most delicious raisins you will ever taste.

Grapes are also sun-dried before they are pressed for wine making, so that the sugar content is greater and thus the alcohol level is higher. All the villages of the Axarquía produce the typical Málaga wine, very much in fashion a century ago until phylloxera struck. Usually it is sweet, but drier vintages are made too. In some cortijos the grapes are still crushed in the age-old way, by hours of treading.

Cómpeta has the widest fame for its wine – it holds a wine fiesta every August 15 in the main square – but every village is convinced that its own product is as good or better.

White-bleached Cómpeta (pop. 2300) spills attractively down its hillside, the domed brick tower of its 16th-century parish church jutting above the tiled rooftops. Despite its distance from the coast, Cómpeta has become a home from home for many Britons and Danes, who have bought abandoned farmhouses on nearby hillsides and renovated them.

Swing right up a steep street to enter the village and reach a car park. Check out Cerámica La Posada, the showroom on the left between the car park and the church square. The friendly English-speaking proprietors stock their own imaginative, high-quality stoneware. Just opposite is La Bodega, a pleasant bar that retains the press once used to crush the grapes.

Bar-Restaurante Perico in the church square is a favourite meeting place, as is El Loro, in the adjacent Plaza Pantaleón. Both serve tapas and meals at reasonable prices.

The village, with its steep crook-leg streets and alleys, is pleasant to walk through and easy to get lost in, especially if you have been sampling the wine. These days, to judge by the mushrooming real estate offices, the biggest local industry is buying and selling property.

Further inland lies Canillas de Albaida (known to the Arabs as "the white one"), where a road plunges into a gorge then climbs to meet the Archez-Salares road.

From Cómpeta you have a choice of routes back to the coast. The more direct one is a scenic 20-kilometre run, via MA111, to Algarrobo Costa, near Torre del Mar. Just after a petrol station look for a monument from the Franco years at the side of the road. It pays tribute to an 18-year-old law student "vilely assassinated by the Marxist hordes on this spot on January 8, 1937".

Passing vineyards, almond and olive trees, you reach Sayalonga and Algarrobo, where a stroll through tortuous streets brings you to the Ermita de San Sebastián for a good view of the village.

An alternative, longer route to the coast from Cómpeta takes you through the mountains and then down to Vélez-Málaga. You will really feel you have hit the back country as you roller-coast through the sierras past a series of remote white villages.

Roll the village names off your tongue... Salares, Sedella, Canillas de Aceituno, all hotbeds of rebellion in the 16th-century Morisco war and still with a Moorish air about them.

Take the MA111 towards Algarrobo and, four kilometres from Cómpeta, fork sharp right into the valley to Archez. A sign indicates the Ruta del Mudéjar.

Archez, a dozy huddle of houses once immersed in poverty and neglect, has been spruced up. It has a remarkable church tower, a 14th century minaret with beautifully ornate brickwork.

Just outside the village, turn right on the MA158, up and over the hill towards tiny Salares, also boasting a fine minaret, and Sedella. On the right rises the great bulk of Maroma, at 2,065 metres the highest peak in Málaga province. Often clothed in snow in winter, it marks the boundary between Málaga and Granada provinces.

Almond and olive trees dot the slopes and citrus orchards occupy more sheltered spots around Canillas de Aceituno (pop. 2700). A footpath weaves up to the summit of Maroma from Canillas. It is a strenuous all-day hike and walkers should be properly equipped – freak storms can lash the heights even in summer.

The first stretch—to the Fuente de la Rábita, a delightful picnic spot—is quite steep but takes only about one hour. The path starts by the fountain alongside the Canillas Ayuntamiento.

After Canillas, the road, now the MA125, executes a few hair-pins before finally dipping down to the C335. Turn left towards the coast. Passing down the Río Vélez valley, you reach Vélez Málaga. Although modern buildings surround it, the atmosphere of old Spain still lingers in the narrow streets hugging the hill below the restored Arab fortress.

Development is fast linking Vélez with nearby Torre del Mar on the main coast highway.

In search of gold

From Cómpeta an excursion along the MA117 towards Vélez Málaga – a road of a thousand curves – brings you to the hamlet of Daimalos and a spring with magical powers. A legend from Moorish times relates that the water of the Fuente Perdida can restore a man's sexual power and a woman's fertility.

Just before the village of Arenas, a track to the left dips into the river bed and then winds up precipitously for three kilometres to Bentomiz castle (not for nervous drivers).

This was an important fortress in the time of the Moors. Almond and olive trees grow within the ruined walls and there are stupendous views, making it an ideal picnic spot.

A huge bell of solid gold reportedly once hung in the castle. When the Christians were about to conquer the fortress, the Moors hid the bell in a tunnel. Treasure-seekers are still looking for it.

*Frigiliana and
the Sierra Almijara*

Drying Grapes

Forest guard

WHAT TO SEE

Archez:
Church tower, a 12th-century minaret.

Canillas de Aceituno:
Magnificent views of Axarquía from the upper quarter; *Casa de la Reina Mora*, Mudéjar tower.

Cómpeta:
Asunción church, neo-Mudéjar tower.

Frigiliana:
Ingenio, 18th-century palace converted into sugar mill; *San Antonio*, 17th-century church.

Salares:
Church tower, 13th-century minaret.

Sayalonga:
Mudéjar parish church, circular cemetery.

Torrox:
Morisco-style streets; remains of Roman fish factory, necropolis (Torrox Costa).

Vélez Málaga:
see Excursion 8

WHERE TO STAY

Archez:
Posada Mesón Mudéjar. Alamo, 6. Tel. 952 55 31 06. Old house and stable converted into charming five-room hostal. €

Cómpeta:
Balcón de Cómpeta, Calle San Antonio, 75. Tel: 952 55 35 35. Excellent views. Air-conditioned double rooms and bungalows with kitchenettes. Pool, tennis. Restaurant. €€-€€€

Frigiliana:
Las Chinas, Plaza Amparo Guerrero, 14. Tel. 952 53 30 73. Small, simple, handy. € *La Posada Morisca*, Loma de la Cruz. Tel: 952 53 41 51. Rural tranquillity in traditional style. Cosy rooms with stoves. Restaurant. €€-€€€

Los Caracoles, Ctra Frigiliana-Torrox, km 4.6. Tel 952 03 06 80. Comfortable rooms and unusual igloo-shaped bungalows. Fine views, pool, restaurant. €€€-€€€€

Sedella:
Casa Pintá. Tel. 952 50 88 77. Modern British-owned hostal. Fine views. Pool. €€

WHERE TO EAT
Archez:
Posada Mesón Mudéjar. Closed Wed. Cosy atmosphere. Serafín and Loli serve local specialities.

Canillas de Aceituno:
La Sociedad, Calle Iglesia, 12. Tel. 952 51 82 92. Friendly bar-restaurant. Local dishes include fennel soup, kid with garlic, stewed rabbit.

Cómpeta:
El Loro, Plaza Pantaleón Romero, 2. Tel. 952 51 60 75. Tapas and hearty local fare.

Pavo Real, Ctra Torrox-Cómpeta, km 9. Tel. 952 11 51 74. Meeting place for local British. Pea soup a speciality.

Frigiliana:
Las Chinas, Plaza Amparo Guerrero, 16. Tel. 952 53 41 35. Excellent price-quality ratio, served by friendly professional Sebastián. Reservation advisable; *El Cerro*, Ctra Frigiliana-Torrox. Closed Tues. Venta, fine views, serving typical robust dishes.

Sedella:
Casa Pintá. Local dishes, English snacks.

MORE INFORMATION
Frigiliana:
Tourist office, Plaza del Ingenio. Tel. 952 53 31 26. Open 10am-2pm. Closed Tues, sometimes Sat.

Vélez Málaga area:
Tourist office, Avda de Andalucía, s/n, Torre del Mar. Tel. 952 54 11 04. Open Mon-Fri 8am-3pm, 5-8pm, Sat & Sun 10am-2pm.

Hot Springs
of the Moors

View across Los Bermejales reservoir to snow-capped Maroma

THIS IS ONE OF THE MOST SPECTACULAR ROADS IN SPAIN. IT TAKES YOU UP INTO WILD SIERRAS AND TO HOT SPRINGS NEAR THE SPLENDIDLY SITUATED TOWN OF ALHAMA DE GRANADA.

AREA: southwest Granada province and the Axarquía (Málaga)
ROUTE: Almuñécar→Otívar→Jayena→Alhama de Granada→ Ventas de Zafarraya→Vélez Málaga→Almuñécar
DISTANCE: 170 kilometres

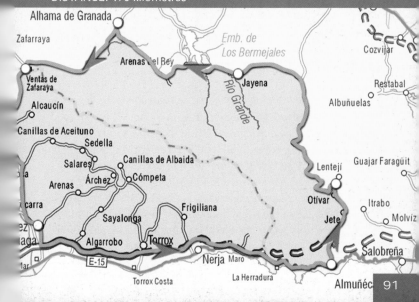

From downtown Almuñécar, head directly inland, crossing the N340 and following signs for Jete and Otívar. You drive up the Río Verde valley on the narrow, tortuous SO2, which winds past lush plantations.

The sheltered conditions allow all manner of exotic fruits to flourish, including custard apples, avocados, medlars, pomegranates and even paw-paws and mangos. Shelves have been cut in the surrounding hillsides to allow more trees to be planted, watered by drip irrigation.

Look for a sign two kilometres from Almuñécar indicating Torre del Monje, Columbario Romano. A steep, stony path past cactus and barking dogs leads to a columbarium, a small square tower inside which are niches where the Romans stored their loved ones' ashes.

Further along, on a right-hand bend at Torrecuevas (3km from Almuñécar), you will see the arches of an aqueduct built by the Romans and still in use.

After the village of Jete, the road climbs the valley side to Otívar (pop. 1200), 14 kilometres from Almuñécar. They still remember the Napoleonic Wars here. A plaque outside the town hall commemorates the courage of a former mayor who stubbornly resisted French invaders.

The quiet streets have evocative names, suggesting past feuds and passions. Look for Calle Beso (kiss street) and Calle Engaño (swindle street).

On the highway running above the village centre, a series of restaurants, balanced on concrete stilts over the abyss, do good business. Specialities, at agreeably low prices, include *morcilla* (black sausage), mountain ham, and chicken cooked with apple. *Vino de la Costa*, served in earthenware jugs, washes it down.

A little beyond Otívar, a side-road zig-zags up four-and-a-half kilometres to Lentejí, a village lodged like an eagle's eyrie 600 metres above sea-level in the Sierra del Chaparral. The pace of life in Lentejí makes Otívar seem like Piccadilly Circus.

Near the Plaza de España and church is the Cueva del Trabuco bar – look for the shotgun – built under the rock. Another bar, the Piedra Dura (hard rock), is down a few steps from the plaza.

Climbing again on the main road, you pass occasional rosemary-and-thyme-covered slopes once clothed in pines. Disastrous fires have destroyed swathes of forest.

The road slices through rock and hairpins upwards to Mirador de la Cabra Montés, a remote petrol station 13 kilometres from Otívar, a worthwhile halt to revel in the splendid views towards the coast. You may even glimpse the wild goats, hawks and eagles that inhabit these lonely sierras.

North of this point the road levels out briefly, then gets really serious. After passing over a narrow saddle between two valleys, it weaves across the face of a sheer cliff before finally reaching a plateau. We pass a farm school and Mesón Los Prados, useful for a snack if it is open. Twenty-eight kilometres after Otívar, turn left amid pinewoods to travel westwards towards Jayena and Alhama de Granada.

If, instead, we stuck to the Granada road, we would soon reach a rolling plain of barley and wheat with the snow-tipped Sierra Nevada shimmering over all. This is a particularly breath-taking sight in springtime.

This road joins the thundering traffic of the Motril-Granada highway at the Suspiro del Moro (Moor's Sigh) pass, so-called because Boabdil, the last Moorish King of Granada, allegedly paused here for a final look at the city from which he had been ousted by the Catholic Monarchs. "Go on, weep like a woman for that which you failed to defend like a man," sniffed his mother.

Few vehicles trundle along the well-paved Jayena road. We head towards Arenas del Rey. Just beyond Fornes, a track to the left leads to La Resinera, a factory once devoted to preparing pine resin, and penetrates the Sierra de Almijara, rising more than 2000 metres. After eight or nine kilometres the valley narrows, a good spot for a picnic by tumbling water.

Continuing towards Arenas and Alhama, you skirt the blue expanse of Los Bermejales, a large reservoir. A short deviation north around the reservoir brings you to the dam on the A338. Near the dam, La Cantina bar offers a cheap menú del día.

West of Arenas, the GR141 runs by fields of corn, dotted with scarlet poppies in spring and early summer. Poplar trees, whose leaves shine like gold coins in autumn, line the river winding down from the sierras towards Alhama de Granada.

Two kilometres before the Alhama-Málaga road, you encounter the Pato Loco restaurant and bar with a swimming pool (open June to September). Next door is El Ventorro hotel. An inn has existed here for centuries - once it was a collecting point for esparto from the sierras.

From Ventorro there's a beautiful walk to Alhama, two kilometres following the Alhama river through a spectacular chasm. The town is magnificently situated below the massive bulk of the Maroma mountain, often snowcapped in winter.

In the past it was important because of its strategic location on the route from Granada to Málaga and renowned for its curative waters - the Arab name Al-hamma means thermal waters.

With luck you can park on the main square near the market. Good drinking water bubbles from the fountain outside the Iglesia del Carmen. Opposite is what remains of Alhama's castle, now a private house sealed off by a high wall.

A short stroll away are the Tajo (gorge) and the main sights, including the parish church which shelters embroidery said to have been executed by Queen Isabel. "You can see it's hers because it is not very good - well, a queen can't be good at everything," explains a local.

In Andalusia's great earthquake of Christmas Day, 1884, several houses tumbled into the chasm. A plaque outside the Encarnación parish church relates that the tremor affected 106 towns and killed 745 people.

On the road to Alhama

Just below the town along the Granada highway, a side-road cuts through a chasm to the Balneario Alhama de Granada, built over 12th-century Moorish baths. The water, gushing from a spring at a temperature of 47 degrees C, is recommended for arthritis, rheumatism, sciatica and breathing problems.

From Alhama it is 19 kilometres over oak-dotted hills to Ventas de Zafarraya. A handy place for refreshment en route is Los Caños de la Alcaicería on a 90-degree bend. A vast fireplace warms the spacious bar, lined with hams.

A fertile valley, hemmed in by rocky heights, leads to Ventas. This was always an important way station for muleteers and stage coaches, for it stands at the head of a pass formed by a narrow gap in the mountains, known as the Boquete de Zafarraya.

Lentejí Basketmaker

Often the pass is shrouded in mist when the sun is shining brightly on the coast. Scenery and climate change quickly as you descend into Málaga province. Occasionally you will glimpse tunnels and an old track where a railway once ran from Málaga up to Ventas de Zafarraya.

As the A335 swings down the valley in wide curves, you pass crumbling walls crowning a hilltop, the ruins of Zalia, a Moorish fortress. A little below the ruins, a turn to the right leads along the C340 to Periana (8km) with fine views over the Viñuela reservoir towards mountains and coast.

Compared to its neighbours, Periana is a youngster, being founded in 1761 and rebuilt after the devastating 1884 earthquake. It is well-known for the quality of its olive oil - follow the green signs indicating the way to the Cooperativa - and its apricots. A delightfully scenic road continues beyond Periana to Ríogordo and Colmenar.

Continuing on the A335 towards Vélez, you see a turn to the left to Puente Don Manuel and - way up on the side of the Sierra de Tejeda - Alcaucín (meaning "the arches" in Arabic), a particularly picturesque village. The murder in the 16th century of the Alcaucín innkeeper and his wife by outlaws provoked such cruel Christian reprisals that the local Moriscos (Moorish converts to Christianity) rose in revolt.

The A335 runs swiftly down towards Vélez Málaga, passing citrus orchards, palm trees, and whitewashed dwellings framed by hibiscus and geraniums. Recently improved, the road bypasses the many hamlets and the village of Viñuela but passes close to the main dam of the Viñuela reservoir.

Sports are being developed on Viñuela's vivid azure waters, which meet the needs of Málaga and the Axarquía. A fine road to the right, the A352, runs across the dam to Los Romanos and Ríogordo, a new highway intended one day to link Marbella and Vélez Málaga.

Alhama de Granada

The road follows the intensely cultivated Vélez river valley and the air grows steadily balmier as we approach the coast. Take a walk through the old quarter of Vélez Málaga (pop. 52,000), the Axarquía's biggest town, to view its sinuous streets and noble buildings. The Moors, who built a fortress here, praised it as "a beautiful city with a fine mosque and an abundance of fruit trees".

Neighbouring Torre del Mar, once a fishing village, is now a prosperous, high-rise resort.

WHAT TO SEE
Alhama:
Iglesia del Carmen, 16th-century church, restored after Civil War damage, fine stonework, Baroque paintings on dome and arches.

Iglesia de la Encarnación, open afternoons (or whenever you can find the priest), Gothic-Renaissance church founded by Catholic Monarchs, museum.

Casa de la Inquisición, interesting facade in Isabelline style on house once used by the Inquisition.

Hospital de la Reina, 15th-century royal hospital with fine coffered ceiling, later a convent, now a library.

Vélez Málaga:
Moorish castle, heavily restored, walk up from Plaza de la Constitución.

Santa María de la Encarnación, 16th-century Mudéjar church overlooking town.

San Juan Bautista, open 10am-1pm, 6-7pm, Gothic church restored in neo-classic style. Casa de Cervantes, open all day, handsome brick-pillared patio, Cervantes apparently stayed here.

Palacio del Marqués de Beniel, 16th century, housing historic archives and Fundación María Zambrano (distinguished thinker born in Vélez).

San Francisco convent, open 7-8pm, founded 1495, minaret, Baroque grandeur. Nuestra Señora de Gracia (Las Claras), open 6-7pm, monastery with Baroque church, nuns sell cakes.

WHERE TO STAY
Alhama de Granada:
Balneario. Tel: 958 35 00 11. Year-round opening planned. Three stars. Spa hotel at thermal springs, with medical supervision for visitors. Facilities being upgraded. €€

El Ventorro, Ctra Játar km2. Tel. 958 35 04 38. Closed 2nd & 3rd week Jan. Small, rustic style hotel. Heating. Hot water maybe. Excursions organised. €€

Los Caños de la Alcaicería, Ctra Alhama-Vélez, km10. Tel. 958 35 03 25. Modern hotel, handily located for hikers, hunters. Pool. €€

La Viñuela:

Hotel La Viñuela, Ctra Vélez-Málaga-Alhama, s/n, La Viñuela. tel. 952 51 91 93. Extensive gardens, pool. Near Viñuela reservoir. Water sports. €€€

Periana:

Villa Turística de la Axarquía, Carril del Cortijo Blanco, Periana. Tel. 952 53 62 22. Village-style hotel in beautiful location, three kilometres from Periana. Tennis, pool. €€€

WHERE TO EAT

Alhama:

Mesón de Diego, Plaza Constitución, 12. Tel. 958 36 01 21. Closed Sat. Rabbit in almond sauce, pork fillet in pepper sauce. Terrace;

El Ventorro. Hearty local dishes;

Los Caños de la Alcaicería, on Ventas de Zafarraya highway. Pork, rabbit, kid grilled on open fire.

La Viñuela:

Hotel La Viñuela. Restaurant offering regional dishes.

Otívar:

Several restaurants offer a local speciality, chicken with apple.

Torre del Mar:

La Cueva, Paseo de Larios, 12. Tel. 952 54 02 23. Ultra-fresh seafood at reasonable prices.

Villa Turística de la Axarquía. Regional dishes.

MORE INFORMATION

Alhama:

Tourism office, Ayuntamiento. Tel. 958 36 06 86. Mon-Fri 11am-3pm.

Vélez Málaga area:

Tourism office, Avda de Andalucía, s/n, Torre del Mar. Tel. 952 54 11 04. Open Mon-Fri 8am-3pm, 5-8pm, Sat &Sun 10am-2pm.

Old Crafts and Prehistoric Paintings

Farmhouse near Grazalema

PREHISTORIC ART, THE HAUNTS OF OUTLAWS AND
EAGLES AND SPLENDID MOUNTAIN SCENERY . . . THE
SERRANÍA DE RONDA Y CÁDIZ HAS MUCH TO OFFER. IT
ALSO BOASTS THE WETTEST PLACE IN SPAIN.

AREA: Sierras of Málaga and Cádiz
ROUTE: Ronda→Montejaque→La Pileta→Cortes de la Frontera →
El Bosque →Ubrique→Grazalema→Ronda
DISTANCE: 124 kilometres

From Ronda we take the A376 highway towards Jerez, branching off after 14 kilometres on the MA505.

Nearing Montejaque, you wind through a chasm with steep cliffs. To your right a wall blocks part of the valley, an example of man's often vain attempts to control nature.

This 60-metre-high dam was built in the 1920s. Unfortunately, the project proved a waste of effort for the dam never filled - the water leaked away through innumerable fissures in the rock.

Near the dam is the large entrance to the Cueva del Hundidero. A stream flows into this cave, runs several kilometres underground then emerges further down the valley in the Cueva del Gato (Cat Cave).

Montejaque boasts of being the prettiest village in these mountains. There are plenty of challengers, but the community has refurbished itself as a centre of rural tourism.

You will find a pleasant tapa bar, Bodega El Rincón, on the Plaza de la Constitución. Here you can sample the black sausage and cured ham for which the Montejaque-Benaoján area is famed. Ask where you can obtain splendid fruit liqueurs, produced by Al-Jaque, a local three-woman cooperative.

Continuing down the Guadiaro valley, we reach the Cueva de la Pileta, 29 kilometres from Ronda. It's not the place for claustrophobes, but it does have some remarkable cave paintings. The entrance is up a rocky hillside in a secluded valley occupied by one farmhouse. One of the Bullón family, who discovered the cave and occupy the house on the flat valley bottom, acts as your guide.

Tours last an hour or more. There is no fancy lighting. Your guide hands you a lamp and you tramp through the dark galleries and the stalactite-and-stalagmite-encrusted caverns, carved out originally by an underground river.

Farmer José Bullón Lobato stumbled across the cave in 1905. He found an opening in the rock and lowered himself on a rope, thinking he might find useful supplies of bat-dung. Instead, he came across innumerable traces of prehistoric man. Skeletons, pottery, and Paleolithic wall paintings were revealed in La Pileta. An archer, a deer, a fish, abstract symbols are among the murals created by early man.

Ten kilometres from the cave is Cortes de la Frontera. This is one of the wettest parts of Andalusia, producing flourishing vegetation, and Cortes is one of the loneliest villages. It lies on the edge of two national parks, Los Alcornales and Grazalema.

Continuing southwest, you swing right on the A373 towards Ubrique. To the west lies the 170,000-hectare Alcornocales park, a wilderness of cork oaks and wild life - keep your eyes open for deer, wildcats, eagles and vultures.

The road climbs steadily, entering Cádiz province. At the Monjón de la Víbora crossroads, there is a breath-taking panoramic view of the Sierra de Cádiz before you swoop down to Ubrique (pop. 18,000) sheltering in the valley at the foot of the Cruz del Tajo mountain.

Despite its isolated position, Ubrique is renowned for the quality of its handworked leather. The industrious inhabitants began making petacas (tobacco pouches) from goat skin, often trading with the smugglers who brought tobacco from Gibraltar.

In the past it achieved a certain notoriety for pirating brand names, but of course this no longer occurs. Now Piel de Ubrique is a luxury item, with an international reputation. Dozens of small workshops turn out handbags and wallets for top brand names. A number of the shops bear the "venta directa" (direct sale) sign. If you want to visit a workshop, inquire at the tourist office.

From Ubrique, you have a choice of two scenic routes to Grazalema. The shorter route is via Benaocaz on the A375. Two kilometres from Ubrique along the A375 look for the sign for the Roman city of Ocuri.

A wealthy farmer, Juan de Vegazo, was the first to throw light on the importance of this strategically located settlement when he bought the land more than 200 years ago. Excavation continues but remains of funeral chambers, cisterns and other public buildings are visible. The reception office has explanatory boards, a cafe and stunning views.

For the longer route to Grazalema, take the A373 north to El Bosque, 16 kilometres away. Just before the Tavizna river, you will see the ruins of Aznalmara castle to your right.

El Bosque (pop. 1800) has important fish hatcheries and is a useful spot to pick up information about the Grazalema Nature Park. There is a park visitors' centre on Avenida de la Diputación, next to the public swimming pool.

From El Bosque the A372 climbs steeply up into the heart of the 51,000-hectare Grazalema nature park. Fork left towards Benamahoma to run below the village to a hatchery where thousands of trout swarm in pools. You can buy them by the kilo.

A hundred yards or so past the trout farm are a bar, restaurant and municipal swimming pool, benefitting from the clear water gushing from the mountains.

As you scale El Boyar pass, 1103 metres high, you enjoy stupendous mountain vistas. In early summer the slopes blaze yellow with gorse blooms. On the heights grows the Abies pinsapo Boiss, a Spanish fir found nowhere else in Europe. It prefers cold, damp places more than 1000 metres above sea level.

Grazalema - a classic white village of cobbled streets, tiled roofs and ironwork balconies - appears, nestling below peaks of up to 1650 metres. Clouds sail in from the Atlantic to collide with these mountains, dumping around 2000 litres per metre of rain per year. Result: Grazalema is said to be the wettest village in Spain.

But the village (pop. 2300) has another claim to fame – its hand-woven woollen goods. The craft was in danger of dying out but has been revived.

At the village entrance, look for the petrol station. Just after, turn right up the hill to the Nuestra Señora del Carmen factory and

Grazalema craftsman

shop, where you can see high-quality blankets and ponchos turned out on 200-year-old looms. A shop on the village plaza also sells its products.

Grazalema is a handy centre for enjoying a series of outdoor activities, from hiking to potholing. And every July you can show off your bravado before a fighting bull that chases through Grazalema's streets during the Lunes del Toro fiesta (the first Monday after the Virgin of Carmen fiesta). Bumps and bruises are not uncommon.

From Grazalema, the A372 winds past holm and holly oaks before joining the A376 to take you back to Ronda.

WHAT TO SEE

Benaoján:

Cueva de La Pileta. Tel. 952 16 73 43. One-hour guided tours starting 10am-1pm, 4-5pm. Entry 6.50 euros.

Ubrique:

Ocuri, Roman ruins. Open 10am-7.30pm, summer 10am-2pm, 8-10pm. Entry 3 euros.

Grazalema:

Nuestra Señora del Carmen, woollen factory. Tel. 956 13 20 08. Open Mon-Thurs 8am-2pm and 3-6.30pm, Fri 8am-2pm.

WHERE TO STAY

Benaoján:

Molino del Santo, Barriada Estación. Tel. 952 16 71 51. British-run two-star hotel in a delightful converted old mill. €€€-€€€€

Cortes de la Frontera:

Soly y Sierra, Avda Sol y Sierra, 1. Tel. 952 15 45 23. Four stars. Luxury amid the mountains. Pool, restaurant, fine views. €€€€

Grazalema:

Villa Turística, El Olivar, s/n, Grazalema, Cádiz. Tel: 956 13 21 36. Built in pueblo style. 176 beds, pool, restaurant;

Puerta de la Villa, Plaza Pequeña, 8. Tel. 956 13 23 76. Four-star hotel. Stylish furnishings, sauna, jacuzzi. €€€€

Casa de las Piedras, Las Piedras, 32. Tel. 956 13 20 14. Friendly hostal located in old village house. €

Lunes del Toro, Grazalema

Montejaque:

Palacete de Mañara, Plaza de la Constitución, 2. Tel. 952 16 72 52. Three-star rustic-style hotel in a 16th-century mansion. €€

Casas de Montejaque, Calle Manuel Ortega, 16. Tel. 952 16 81 20. Some 30 village houses available for rent.

WHERE TO EAT

Benaoján:

Molino del Santo restaurant. Tel: 952 16 71 51. Good food, friendly service. Willow-tree-shaded terrace beside rushing mountain stream.

El Bosque:

Hotel Las Truchas, Avda. Diputación, 1. Tel: 956 71 60 61. Fresh trout.

Jimera de Líbar:

Quercus. See Excursion 2.

Grazalema:

Casa de las Piedras. Local dishes served.

Montejaque:

Palacete de Mañara restaurant. Local specialities.

MORE INFORMATION

Grazalema:

Tourism office Tel. 956 13 22 25. Open 10am-2pm, 5-7pm. Closed Mon.

Ubrique:

Tourist office, Avenida Morena de Mora, 19. Tel. 956 46 49 00. Open daily 10am-2pm, 4.30-7.30pm.

El Bosque:

Centros de Visitantes, Parque Natural de Grazalema: Avenida de la Diputación, 13, El Bosque. Tel. 956 71 60 63. Open Mon-Fri 10am-2pm, Oct-March 4-6pm, April Sept 6-8pm; Avenida de la Democracia, Cortes de la Frontera. Tel. 952 15 45 99.

Mountain Fortresses
and Roman Ruins

A mighty gorge splits the town of Ronda

JUST INLAND FROM THE COSTA DEL SOL LIE SOME OF
SPAIN'S WILDEST SCENERY AND MOST SPECTACULAR
TOWNS. THIS TOUR TAKES YOU TO SCENES OF ANCIENT
BATTLE, ROMAN RUINS AND A VILLAGE THAT APPEARS
ABOUT TO BE CRUSHED BETWEEN JAWS OF ROCK.

AREA: Mountains of Málaga and Cádiz
ROUTE: Ronda→Zahara→Olvera→Seteníl→Ronda La Vieja→Ronda
DISTANCE: 110 kilometres

The journey starts in Ronda, once the capital of a small Moorish kingdom. Balanced on the edge of a 200-metre-deep chasm, the town is regarded as the birthplace of modern bullfighting. Its sights include old palaces, Arab baths, the bullring opened in 1785 and a variety of museums.

You take the Seville road, the A376. The road crosses the railway line to Algeciras and the Río Guadiaro. Twenty kilometres from Ronda, branch left to take a winding road to Zahara de la Sierra. You run alongside the Guadalcín reservoir before forking left towards the cluster of dwellings.

A tower sprouts from a crag above Zahara, surely one of the most dramatically situated in all Andalusia. From the village centre you can take a steep walk up to the fortress for fine views of olive groves, bare hills, and the town of Olvera cresting a rise in the distance.

Imagine the scene back in the 15th century when this was a Moorish stronghold on the borders of the kingdom of Granada. Christian forces captured it, but one night during a wild storm Muley Hacen, King of Granada, killed the soldiers manning the fortress and marched off with a bunch of captives. This incident backfired. The Castilian warlords were so incensed that they redoubled their efforts against the Moors. The attack on Zahara helped ensure the fall of Granada itself.

Zahara (pop. 1500) is a useful centre for exploring the adjacent mountains. An information office in the centre can organise horse riding, mountain biking and other activities. Ask there about visiting the Garganta Verde, a spectacular gorge. Numbers are limited to 30 a day to avoid disturbing the griffon vultures (*buitres leonados*) there and during the nesting season permission to enter is required.

The Garganta lies five kilometres south of Zahara off the CA531. A road side sign warns that it is a "very tough" two-kilometre excursion; in fact, the first 500 metres are not too difficult, leading to a chamber in the rock known as the Ermita. However, traversing the rest of the narrow gorge is for experienced, rope-equipped climbers only.

If you continue on the CA531, it soars and loops spectacularly as it wends its way to Grazalema (see Excursion 9). Vultures and hawks circle over the heights.

From Zahara drive north to the A382 Antequera-Arcos road and turn right. Soon you will see the majestic outline of Olvera (pop. 5000) away to the left. There's an arrogant air about this town, riding a lofty ridge, surmounted by castle and church. You understand why somebody once wrote: "Olvera, one street, one church, one castle... but what a Street, what a Church, what a Castle!"

The main street itself is quite something. It runs uphill for ever, finally reaching the Plaza de la Iglesia. Here stands Encarnación church, built over a mosque in the 14th century and rebuilt by the Duque de Osuna two centuries later with two imposing bell-towers. There is a Gothic baptismal chapel.

María, at Number 2, Plaza de la Iglesia, has the key for the church. María really is a key figure around here - until recently you had to walk through her living room in order to gain access to the 12th-century Arab castle. Now you enter the fortress via the tourist information office. From the battlements the panorama is tremendous, but don't go up if you have no head for heights.

Just below the plaza stands the town hall, which dates back to 1783. Note: there is very little parking space at the top of the town, so it is better to leave your car lower down and hike up.

Between Olvera and Bornos, away to the west, a section of disused railway line has been converted into a "green trail", a track for the use of hikers and cyclists.

From Olvera we head southeast to Setenil, one of the strangest and most claustrophobic towns in Andalusia. It is only 15 kilometres away, but finding the start of the road can be difficult. It runs under the A382 bypass around Olvera.

You pass the village of Torre-Alháquime. A tour company based here recreates a bit of history by offering tourists the chance to be kidnapped by outlaws. A dramatic rescue is followed by fiery flamenco dancing and lots of food and drink.

Fields of barley and asparagus flourish in the fertile valley where Torre lies. The road weaves over the hills and, finally, Setenil appears, wedged into a crevice. Penetrate this village and you discover that the locals have devised a clever way of cutting building costs. Many houses have been created by simply erecting walls so that overhanging shelves of rock form the roof.

This has been the custom since medieval times and the villagers happily continue living in their rocky abodes. No doubt frequent prayers to the Virgin ensure that they will never suffer any earth tremors.

Take time to stroll the sinuous streets of Setenil as far as the Iglesia Mayor and the remains of its castle in the upper part of town.

If you head out of town on a road that leads westwards to Villalones and El Gastor, after a few kilometres you encounter a narrow side-road to the left. Marked as MA486, this curves uphill to Acinipo, otherwise known as Ronda La Vieja. It takes you to ruins spectacularly situated on a lofty ridge, with magnificent views over the sierras.

Traces have been found of circular dwellings dating back to the eighth century BC. In Roman times there was an important settlement here, the most striking evidence of which is a semi-circular theatre believed to have been constructed 1900 years ago.

Acinipo is one of the spots where Julius Caesar and Pompey are said to have fought the Battle of Munda around 45BC, but there does not seem to be much historical proof of this.

All around are piles of stones from the vanished settlement, deposited there over centuries as farmers cleared the land for ploughing. Many stones ended up as building material for the houses of Ronda.

From Acinipo, the MA449 meanders downhill to join the A376 which will return you to Ronda.

Setenil houses are wedged beneath shelves of rock.

WHAT TO SEE

Olvera:
Castle, open 10am-2pm, 5-7pm, closed Mon.

Encarnación church, built over a mosque in the 14th century.

Ronda:
Plaza de Toros, open 10am-6pm, Spain's oldest bullring, with bullfight museum.

Puente Nuevo and *El Tajo*, chasm spanned by a two-centuries-old bridge. Santa María la Mayor, open 10am-6pm, church built over mosque on King Fernando the Catholic's orders.

Palacio de Mondragón, open Mon-Fri 10am-6pm, Sat-Sun 10am-3pm, built 1314, municipal museum.

Baños Arabes (Arab Baths), open Tues 9.30am-1.30pm, 4-6pm, Wed-Sat 9.30am-3.30pm, closed Sun, Mon.

Casa del Rey (Moorish King's House), open 10am-7pm.

Museo del Bandolero, Calle Armiñán, 65, open 10am-7pm, weapons, photos, documents associated with sierra outlaws.

Ronda La Vieja (Acinipo). Open Tues-Sun 10am-5pm. Closed Mon pm. Hours can change, call 630 42 99 49 to check. Roman ruins, mighty views.

Setenil:
Houses built under the rock.

Zahara de la Sierra:
Remains of Moorish castle; *Garganta Verde*, spectacular gorge, call Grazalema Nature Park office in El Bosque re entry permit, 956 72 70 29.

WHAT TO DO

Ronda:
Balloon flights, dawn take-off to view Ronda and sierras.
Tel. 952 87 72 49.

Torre Alháquime (Cádiz):
Bandit adventure, Bandoleros Tours, Plaza de la Constitución, 1.
Tel. 956 12 51 24.

WHERE TO STAY

Olvera:

Sierra y Cal, Avda Nuestra Señora de los Remedios 2, Tel: 956 13 03 03. Handy budget overnight. Rooms have heating. Restaurant. €

Ronda:

Alavera de los Baños, Calle San Miguel, s/n. (next to Baños Arabes). Tel. 952 87 91 43. Arches, tiles and colours give Moorish feel to charming small hostal. €€-€€€

Parador, Plaza de España. Tel: 952 87 75 00. In a magnificent situation on the edge of the gorge, the three-storey parador opened in 1994. €€€€

El Horcajo, Ctra Ronda-Zahara de la Sierra, km 95.5, Ronda. Tel. 952 18 40 80. Old farmhouse converted into a three-star hotel. Large grounds. Fine views. Pool. €€€

Zahara de la Sierra:

Marqués de Zahara, San Juan, 3. Tel: 956 12 30 61. Two-star hostal. Spartan but clean. Restaurant. €

WHERE TO EAT

Olvera:

Sierra y Cal's Restaurant offers local dishes including stewed venison and pork fillet stuffed with chorizo.

Ronda:

El Escudero, Paseo de Blas Infante, 1. Tel. 952 87 13 67. Old mansion with view of gorge. Andalusian cuisine; many tapa bars including Bodega La Verdad (sherry and Málaga wine from barrel) and Bar Portón in Pedro Romero alley near bullring.

MORE INFORMATION

Olvera:

Tourism office, Plaza de la Iglesia. Tel. 956 12 08 16. Open 10am-2pm, 5-7pm. Closed Mon.

Zahara:

Sierra de Grazalema Visitors' Centre, Plaza de Zahara 3. Tel. 956-12 31 14. Open daily 9am-2pm, 4-7pm, Sun pm closed.

Ronda:

Tourism office, Paseo de Blas Infante, s/n. Tel. 952 18 71 19. Open Mon-Fri 9.30am-6.30pm, Sat-Sun 10am-2pm, 3.15-6.30.

Puente Nuevo Interpretation Centre, open Mon-Fri 10am-6pm, Sat-Sun 10am-3pm.

Olvera

Ronda's Plaza de Toros, Spain's oldest bullring.

Ronda Bullfight Museum

Seafood, Sherry and Flamenco

SHERRY LAND IS THE PLACE WHERE ALL THE STEREOTYPES ABOUT SOUTHERN SPAIN SEEM TO FIT. FIERY FLAMENCO DANCERS, LAND-OWNING ARISTOCRATS, SUPERB HORSES, FIGHTING BULLS, PRETTY GIRLS AND FINE WINE. . . THEY ARE ALL HERE.

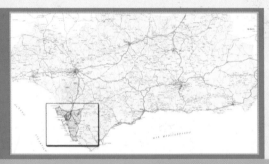

AREA: Province of Cádiz
ROUTE: Jerez→Sanlúcar→El Puerto→Vejer→Medina Sidonia →Arcos →Jerez
DISTANCE: 230km

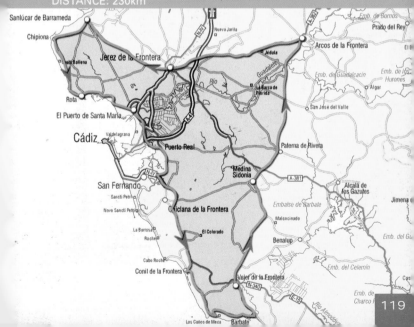

11 Seafood, Sherry and Flamenco

This excursion takes you around the Sherry Triangle, formed by Jerez de la Frontera, Puerto de Santa María and Sanlúcar de Barrameda, but also takes in sleepy whitewashed towns, Atlantic beaches and the hilltop fortress of Arcos de la Frontera.

Jerez (pop. 190,000) is a modern city, but its pleasant old quarter offers palatial dwellings and impressive churches. It is dominated by the industry that made it famous.

The Moors called this place "Scheris" and from this came the name "Jerez". British names and links abound among the sherry families, although most of the great bodegas (wineries) are now run by multinational companies.

Atlantic breezes, wet winters, hot summers and the chalky soil combine with centuries of expertise to produce sherry. Visit a bodega to view the time-honoured solera system. New wine is blended with older wines by decanting it through a series of barrels —Jerez has a million 500-litre casks of American oak.

Vino fino (dry, pale and best served chilled) usually goes through more blending stages than sherries with more body, such as *amontillados* (nutty-flavoured and deeper-coloured) and *olorosos* (darker still and full-bodied).

For a dazzling display of horsemanship, visit the Real Escuela Andaluza del Arte Ecuestre, where the "dancing horses of Andalusia" are put through their paces. The Jerez Feria del Caballo in May is a must for horse fanciers.

Jerez is also noted for its flamenco performers and aficionados can find books, music and dance classes at the Andalusian Flamenco Foundation.

Take the A480 from Jerez towards Sanlúcar de Barrameda, 23 kilometres away. Regiments of vines march over rolling hills. Palomino grapes predominate in the making of *finos* and *amontillados*. The dazzling white soil is albariza - its high percentage of chalk, plus clay and sand, absorbs moisture well and then, under the baking sun, forms a hard crust to retain it.

Sanlúcar at the mouth of the Guadalquivir river lives from fishing and wine. A plaque on the Ayuntamiento wall records that, of 265 men who sailed from here with Magellán on September 20, 1519, to voyage around the world, only 18 returned three years later. About to embark on another epic voyage, Columbus had to delay his ships' departure from Sanlúcar because his crew insisted on joining the Rocío pilgrimage in the Guadalquivir marshlands.

From Sanlúcar's bodegas comes *manzanilla*, a light dry sherry with a delicate flavour created, it is said, by the sea breezes wafting over the maturing wine. *Manzanilla*, served from the barrel in the many bars, is ideal to drink with tapas.

Check out the bars around the palm-shaded central square, the Plaza del Cabildo. Casa Balbino offers everything from stuffed squid to sea snails. It is presided over by four brothers, Antonio, Joaquín, Balbino and Elías - and the head of a 475-kilo bull killed by matador Paco Ojeda to mark the opening of Seville's Expo 92.

Fresh seafood, sometimes cooked with sherry, is the speciality of this region. Try *urta a la roteña* (sea-bream cooked with brandy, peppers, tomato, thyme and white wine), *tortillitas de camarones* (shrimp pancakes), *puntillitas* (baby squid), and *galeras* (large crunchy shrimps).

Langostinos (king prawns) are a speciality in the eating places along the Bajo de Guía, the fishermen's district by the river, spruced up with a fine promenade. Tasty *acedías* (small flounder) and *pijotas* (whiting) are a lot cheaper.

On the far shore is the Doñana National Park. You can only enter on a guided tour. A boat, named the Real Fernando after the first steamboat built in Spain that plied the river from 1817, takes visitors across to make short walks with guides. Visits to the park can also be made starting at El Acebuche, Huelva province (see Excursion 19).

Sanlúcar is the home of the Duchess of Medina Sidonia. Among her ancestors were the legendary warrior Guzmán el Bueno and the duke who commanded the Invincible Armada against England.

Three kilometres along the Guadalquivir river bank from Sanlúcar is Bonanza, once a port much used for trade with the Indies. Arrive around 4 or 5pm and you will see vast catches of fish being unloaded and auctioned.

Nine kilometres west of Sanlúcar lies Chipiona. Holidaymakers flood its beaches in summer. Rocío Jurado, queen of Spanish popular song, was born here. Look for her statue near the fishing harbour. A pleasant place to watch the sun sink into the Atlantic is the esplanade by the Chipiona lighthouse.

Continue south via A491. The coast has long, sandy beaches but can be windy. Mass tourism is catered for at Costa Ballena, a huge new complex of apartments, hotels and golf course promoted by the Andalusian government.

Rota's name is mostly associated with its large naval base (under Spanish control but with a big U.S. presence). But it also has a pleasant old quarter, an excellent beach and a fishing port.

The magnificent 13th-century Castillo de Luna—the Catholic Monarchs stayed here in 1477, Franco in 1953—has been restored to house the town hall. On a wall is a plaque to Bartolomé Pérez, of Rota, one of the crew in Columbus's first voyage.

Opposite the castle is a beautiful Gothic church, Santa María de la O. An inscription on the church wall tells how in the prolonged drought of 1917 the Rota people took the image of Jesus out in procession "when the sky immediately darkened and a copious rain providentially fell".

The A491 runs east, skirting the naval base perimeter fence. Ignore signs pointing to Puerto Sherry, a large pleasure port, and continue to El Puerto de Santa Maria (pop. 70,000). This rival to Jerez is famed for its matadors, seafood and bodegas. It also claims to have 800 bars.

It was called The City of 100 Palaces when trade with the Indies flourished and merchants built splendid mansions. Look for the fountain on the Plaza de Las Galeras, where galleons took on water for Atlantic voyages.

This is in the Ribera del Marisco area on the Guadalete river waterfront—a great spot for ultra-fresh seafood. *Ortiguillas* (sea anenome) and *cazón* (shark) are among local specialities. Take your pick at a *cocedero*, a sort of takeaway, then carry them, wrapped in paper, to a pavement cafe table. Chilled dry sherry washes the food down.

The Puerto's bodegas include Terry and Osborne. All across Spain you will see silhouetted on hilltops big replicas of the black Osborne bull. Attempts to remove them in 1994 provoked a national outcry and they were reprieved.

From El Puerto take the highway south, glimpsing Cádiz on a peninsula away to the right. You pass a wilderness of salt flats and fish farms and continue on the N340 past Chiclana to Conil de la Frontera, an unassuming town with mostly Spanish visitors.

In Conil follow the much-improved seafront south to the river, then head inland, and cross a bridge to take a minor road to El Palmar and Los Caños de Meca. Soon you sight a lighthouse on a headland. This is Cape Trafalgar. Near here on October 21, 1805, Nelson routed the Franco-Spanish fleet—only to succumb to his wounds.

Good beaches at Los Caños attract crowds in summer, including nudists. Windsurfers find excellent conditions. Until recently a hippy haven, it is moving upmarket and developers have big plans.

A road curls up through pinewoods to reach Barbate, eight kilometres away. This somewhat bleak town has a new promenade and cleaned-up beach. Tuna fishing has been big business here since Guzmán el Bueno was granted the fishing rights.

Two kilometres or so off-shore, huge anchors retain a wall of netting which in spring and early summer funnels migrating bluefin tuna into a killing zone. Tuna steak is on many local menus and slices of *mojame* (salted tuna) are on sale.

Inland stands a beautifully-located *pueblo blanco*, Vejer de la Frontera. From a distance it appears to be a snow-capped hill.

11 Seafood, Sherry and Flamenco

Along Vejer's esplanade, commanding views of rolling countryside, a wall plaque proclaims:"Vejer! If you were a woman, I would fall in love with you."

From Vejer, head along the A393 through undulating, bull-raising pastures to Medina Sidonia, another archetypal hilltop town, 26 kilometres away. Dating back to Phoenician and Roman times, it offers fine views from the ruins of the Arab fort. Nearby is the Gothic-Mudéjar church of Santa María (La Coronada), with an outstanding Baroque altarpiece. The gossip centre is the spacious Plaza de España, with a handsome town hall.

The A393 carries on 38 kilometres to Arcos de la Frontera. The first sight of the town perched on a cliff above the Guadalete river is breath-taking. Allegedly founded by a grandson of Noah, Arcos once controlled a small Moorish kingdom and was later on the frontier between warring Moors and Christians.

Driving is difficult, so park your car and climb the tortuous, claustrophobic streets to the Plaza del Cabildo, where a *mirador* offers dazzling views. On one side is the castle, still a private residence. Also on the square is Santa María church; climb the tower for a dizzy view. Excellent tapas and good flamenco music are offered at Bar Alcaraván, a dungeon under the castle. Or try the jasmine-perfumed terrace of El Casino.

Semana Santa is particularly spectacular in this medieval atmosphere. Locals claim that the house walls lean inwards in the hope that they will be touched by passing crosses. On Easter Sunday a bull is released to chase the more daring through the old quarter.

The A382 leads back to Jerez. Just before the Jerez Grand Prix circuit, observe on the right Mesón La Cueva, near the tower of Melgarejo castle. The modern building stands over a cave once used as an inn. Legend has it that the innkeepers, having accidentally killed a drunken customer, chopped him up and tossed the pieces into a well. Visitors get a friendlier welcome today at La Cueva, recommended for food and lodging.

WHAT TO SEE

Jerez:

Real Escuela Andaluza de Arte Ecuestre, Recreo de las Cadenas, Avenida Duque de Abrantes. "Dancing horses" show noon Thurs, also noon Tues March-Oct. Entry 12-18 euros. Training sessions weekday mornings.

Centro Andaluz de Flamenco, Palacio Pemartín, Plaza San Juan, 1. Tel. 956 34 92 65. Open Mon-Fri 9am-2pm. Audiovisual show, exhibitions.

Alcázar,12th-century fortress open May-Sept 15, 10am-8pm, Sept 16-April, 10am-6pm, summer Sun, 10am-3pm.

Cathedral, open Mon-Fri 11am-1pm, 6-8pm, Sun 11am-2pm, Gothic, Baroque, Neo-classical styles.

Churches of San Dionisio (Mudéjar), *Santiago* (Gothic 15th century), *Santo Domingo* (Gothic cloister).

La Cartuja, 4km from town, Gothic monastery, magnificent Baroque facade, patio & gardens. Open Mon-Sat, 9.30-11.15am, 12.45-6.30pm.

Sanlúcar:

Nuestra Señora de la O, Plaza Condes de Niebla, Gothic-Baroque, guided visits 10.30am, 11.30am, 12.30pm, daily except Thurs.

Palacio de Orleáns y Borbón, now town hall, Cuesta de Belén, s/n, open mornings, except Thurs, from 10am.

Castillo de Santiago, square-towered 15th-century castle overlooking town and river.

Doñana National Park – boat trip and guided tour on foot, morning and afternoon April-October, mornings only September-March, reserve tickets at Centro de Visitantes, Bajo de Guía, tel. 956 36 38 13. Tour by four-wheel-drive, Tues & Fri, Viajes Doñana, tel. 956 36 25 40. Centro de Interpretación, Bajo de Guía, exhibition, Wed-Sat 10am-2pm, 4-7pm, Sun 10am-2.30pm.

Rota:

Castillo de Luna, guided visits Sat & Sun; Nuestra Señora de la O, 9am-1pm, 6.30-9pm, guided visit Wed 11am.

Castillo de San Marcos – castle on site of a 12th-century Moorish mosque and fortress. Open 10am-2pm. Closed Mon.

Plaza de Toros – century-old bullring. Open 11am-1.30pm, 6-7.30pm, closed Mon.

Fundación Rafael Alberti, Calle Santo Domingo, 25. Poet's childhood home, poems, paintings, Mon-Fri 10.30-2.30pm.

Bahía de Cádiz, El Vapor ferry runs several times a day across bay to Cádiz.

Arcos:
Santa María, Gothic-Plateresque 15th-century church on site of a mosque. Open: Mon-Fri 10am-1pm, 3.30-6.30pm, Sat 10am-2pm; San Pedro, Gothic church. Open: Open: Mon-Sat 10am-1pm, 4-7pm, Sun 10am-1.30pm.

Bolonia:
Baelo Claudia, Bolonia bay - Roman settlement 42km southeast of Vejer via N340. Temples, streets, forum, theatre. Visits Tues-Sat 10am-5.30pm, Sun 10am-1.30pm. Closed Mon. Information: 956-68 85 30.

Sailboarders flock to windswept Tarifa, 15km further south, on the Straits of Gibraltar.

Jerez Grape Harvest

Jerez:

At least 10 wineries welcome visitors, including *González Byass, John Harvey, Pedro Domecq, Williams and Humbert,* and *Sandeman* (inquire details at tourism office). Entrance charge. Booking recommended.

Puerto de Santa Maria

Wineries here can be visited by prior arrangement, including *Osborne,* Calle de los Moros. Mon-Fri, 1pm, 3pm Spanish, 10.30am, 1.30pm English. Call 956 86 91 00 at least 24 hours before; *Terry,* Toneleros, s/n, mornings, call 956 54 36 90; *Grant,* Calle Bolos, 1, Mon-Fri 12.30-1.30pm, call 956 87 04 06, Sat 12.30pm without prior arrangement; *501,* Calle Valdés, 9, June, July, Sept Mon-Fri 12am. Tel: 956 85 55 11.

Sanlúcar:

Visits at 12.30pm to *La Cigarrera* (Mon-Tues), *Antonio Barbadillo* (Wed-Thurs), *Pedro Romero* (Fri-Sat). Information at Eurotur 956 38 30 32.

Serving wine at a Jerez bodega

Los Caños de Meca, Cádiz

WHERE TO STAY

Arcos:

Parador Casa del Corregidor, Plaza Cabildo. Tel: 956 70 05 00. Beautiful views. Restaurant with regional dishes. €€€-€€€€

Los Olivos, San Miguel, 2. Tel: 956 70 08 11. Friendly establishment in restored old Andalusian house. €€

La Casa Grande, Maldonado, 10. Tel. 956 70 39 30. Delightful, 18th-century, cliff-edge house tastefully restored. €€€

Caños de Meca:

Alhambra, Ctra Caños de Meca 9.5km. Tel. 956 43 72 16. Moorish arches, friendly atmosphere. €-€€

Fortuna, Avda Trafalgar, 34. Tel. 956 43 70 75. Open March-Nov. Near beach. Upgrading to two-star hotel. €

Puerto de Santa María: Monasterio San Miguel, Larga, 27. Tel. 956 54 04 40. Four-star luxury. Beautiful converted 18th-century monastery. €€€€

Feria de Caballo

Rota:

Duque de Nájera, Gravina, s/n. Tel: 956 84 60 20. Modern, seafront luxury hotel. Restaurant Embarcadero recommended. €€€€

Sanlúcar:

Posada del Palacio, Caballeros, 11. Tel. 956 36 48 40. Two stars. 19th-century mansion with beautiful patio. €€-€€€

Tartaneros, CalleTartaneros, 8. Tel. 956 38 53 78. Dignified converted mansion. €€-€€€

Vejer:

Convento de San Francisco, Plazuela, s/n. Tel. 956 45 10 01. Charming restored 17th-century convent. Recommended restaurant. €€€

WHERE TO EAT

Jerez:
Good tapas at Bar Juanito and others on *Pescadería Vieja*, off Plaza Arenal;

La Mesa Redonda, Manuel de la Quintana, 3. Tel: 956 34 00 69. Closed Sun, holidays and August. Classy, intimate atmosphere. Seasonal specialities.

Venta Antonio, Ctra Jerez-Sanlúcar km 5. Tel. 956 14 05 35. Famed for seafood.

Sanlúcar:
Excellent tapas at such bars as *Casa Balbino*, Plaza del Cabildo, and *Los Caracoles*, Barrio Alto. Popular seafood restaurants along the Bajo de Guía include *Casa Bigote*, *Casa Juan* and *Mirador de Doñana*.

Vejer:
Venta Pinto, La Barca de Vejer (just off the N340): Rustic style, not so rustic prices.

Puerto:
Cocederos such as *Cervecería Romerijo, Ribera del Marisco*, offer fresh shellfish and fried fish; Many tapa bars (ask tourist office for their list);

La Goleta, Ctra de Fuentebravia, km 0.75 (towards Rota). Tel. 956 85 42 32. Closed Mon except summer, Nov 1-15. Intimate restaurant. Fish baked in salt.

Caños de Meca:
El Caña, Avda Trafalgar. Tel. 956 43 73 98. Open April-Oct. Popular terrace overlooking beach. Seafood.

Medina Sidonia:
El Castillo, Ducado de Medina Sidonia. Tel. 956 41 08 23. Roast lamb, pheasant, venison.

Arcos:
El Convento, Marqués de Torresoto, 7. Tel. 956 70 32 22. In an old palace. Try "faisan al paraíso" (pheasant cooked with wine).

MORE INFORMATION

Jerez:
Tourism office, Alameda Christina, 7. Tel. 956 33 11 50. Open Mon-Fri 9.30am-2.30pm, 4.30-6.30pm, Sat 10am-2pm, 4-6pm, Sun 9.30am-3.30pm.

Puerto:
Tourism office, Luna, 22. Tel. 956 54 24 13. Open 10am-2pm, Oct-May 5.30-7.30pm, June-Sept 6-8pm.

Rota:
Tourism office, Castillo de Luna, Calle Cunal, 2. Tel: 956 84 63 45. Open: 10am-2pm, 6-9pm, winter 9am-2pm, 5-9pm.

Sanlúcar:
Tourism office, Calzada del Ejército, s/n. Tel. 956 36 61 10. Open: 9am-2pm, 6-8pm, Sat & Sun 10am-2pm, 6-8.30pm. Winter: 10am-2pm 5-7pm, Sat & Sun 10am-1.30pm, 4-6.30pm.

Medina Sidonia:
Tourism office, Plaza de la Iglesia Mayor. Tel. 956 41 24 04. Open daily 10.30am-2pm, 4-6.30pm.

Arcos:
Tourism office, Plaza del Cabildo, s/n. Tel. 956 70 22 64. Open 10am-3pm, 4-8.30pm, winter 10am-7pm, Sun 10.30am-3pm.

The Old Road
to Granada

Montefrío, one of Andalusia's most spectacularly situated village

FOLK IN A HURRY TAKE THE FAST AUTOROUTE FROM MÁLAGA TO GRANADA. BUT WE LUCKY ONES HAVE TIME TO APPRECIATE MAGNIFICENT MOUNTAIN SCENERY, VISIT BANDITS' HAUNTS, LUNCH BY A TEEMING TROUT STREAM, AND MAKE FASCINATING DETOURS. THAT'S BECAUSE WE ARE TAKING THE OLD ROAD TO GRANADA.

AREA: Eastern Málaga province and Granada province
ROUTE: Málaga→Colmenar →Alfarnate→Riofrío→Loja →Montefrio →Granada
DISTANCE: 170 kilometres

This route takes us to within sight of the fabled Alhambra, but you can easily branch back via the auto route to Málaga at various points.

The old road, the C345, leaves Málaga on the Camino de Colmenar, a continuation of Calle Cristo de la Epidemia, passing the San Miguel cemetery on the left and passing under the N340 auto route. Look for signs to Colmenar and Loja.

The road spirals upwards, at two points running through a tunnel and doing a 360-degree loop to pass over itself. This area is part of the Montes de Málaga, until the late 19th century renowned for their vineyards. Málaga wine, sweet and potent, was internationally popular. But the dreaded phylloxera, a small bug, killed off the vines and delivered a deadly blow to the Málaga wine industry from which it has never fully recovered.

It is worth halting to look back to Málaga and the coast far below. Numerous ventas dot the route. At weekends, particularly during the winter months, thousands of *malagueño* families trek up here to enjoy long, noisy lunches.

Málaga folk say the further you travel from the city the better the food. Cheap and cheerful eating is the order here in no-frills surroundings. The hubbub is part of the fun. A popular dish is the *plato montes*, a gut-filling, cholesterol-heavy plateful of fried peppers, chips, sausage, egg and other ingredients, washed down with *vino del monte*, Málaga wine from the barrel.

Opposite the ventas El Mijeño and El Boticario (just after the 553km marker), you can detour by turning left along a dirt track and plunging into the 4900-hectare Montes de Málaga nature park. A forestation programme has transformed the rolling hills which are carpeted in pines, oaks, olives, carobs, cypresses, poplars and many shrubs, from spiny broom to asparagus ferns.

Down the track on the left, look for vultures in the cages of the Boticario, where sick or rescued animals are cared for. The dusty but well-maintained track continues 10 kilometres to the

Humaina hotel and a recreation area, then climbs back to the highway. The Montes park offers hiking trails and the chance to see foxes, badgers, wild cats, chameleons and other wild life. Short-toed eagles, barn owls, kestrels, and partridge are among the bird species.

Continuing upwards on the C345, you pass the Fuente de la Reina (a track runs 3.8km from here to the Humaina) and climb over the Puerto del León, 960 metres above sea level. Look for a turning to the left that leads to a recreation area and the Lagar de Torrijos, 1.7km down a dirt track. Here there is an *ecomuseo*, an old mill housing equipment for pressing grapes and a display of artefacts used to produce bread and olive oil.

The C345 continues amid broad vistas of cornfields backed by bare, eroded summits, bypassing Colmenar (pop. 3000), a typical white village with the parish church tower rising above tiled rooftops. The name Colmenar (meaning "beehive") is said to derive from the local people's enthusiasm for beekeeping.

For fine views head to the top of the town where the Ermita de la Candelaria stands near a forest of antennas. The structure was founded in 1719 by some Canary Island sailors and later became a convent. Apparently the sailors prayed to the Virgin for deliverance when a storm threatened their boat off Málaga. Miraculously, they survived and, following a promise they had made, they dedicated a chapel to the Virgin.

Near Colmenar lies Riogordo, celebrated for its Easter Week passion play in which hundreds of villagers take part. From Riogordo you can make a detour to one of Andalusia's most amazingly situated villages. Take the MA159 towards Vélez Málaga and look for signs pointing up the mountain to Comares (see Excursion 6).

The A356 runs northwest from Colmenar. Soon a right fork takes you towards Loja along the MA115, which weaves upwards through craggy country, past a massive black rock known as the Tajo de Gomer.

At a junction, where roads lead off to Alfarnate and Alfarnatejo, stands the Venta de Alfarnate, a beamed and whitewashed structure that has accommodated travellers for centuries. This lonely venta claims to be the oldest inn in Andalusia, dating back to 1691.

Outlaws often robbed travellers in this area and, during the 1940s, leftwing rebels vainly challenging Franco's dictatorship hid out in the mountains. A wall plaque notes that on April 21, 1850, at this point 12 armed men ambushed the mail on its way to Málaga and stole important documents.

One of the 19th century's most notorious bandits, El Tempranillo - he boasted "The king may reign in Spain, but in the sierra I do" - is also said to have paid a visit. He could be a little short-tempered, as the inn's owner and diners discovered. Displeased at his cool reception, he forced them at gunpoint to chew their wooden spoons.

At weekends the inn's many rooms and patio are usually crowded with trippers, local girls hurrying between the tables to serve smoked pork and baby goat stew. Those with mega-appetites should order *huevos a la bestia*, a mighty dish of local specialities.

From the venta the road climbs again to Los Alazores pass, 1040 metres up, and once past the border of Granada province becomes the A341. We follow the cultivated valley of the Río Frío, the Sierra Gorda soaring 1671 metres to our right. Olive and almond trees clothe the slopes.

It is time for lunch and Riofrío is nearby. Turn left on the main Seville-Granada highway, the A92. A short distance along you will see a sign to the right, which leads you under the highway to the hamlet of Riofrío.

Near to where rainbow and common trout idle in the clear river water stands a fish nursery with thousands of hatchlings growing fat in the tanks. The nursery also rears sturgeon and has started harvesting their eggs.

It's no surprise to find trout is the speciality in the pleasantly rustic eating places, which numbered 11 at the last count. Prices are very reasonable and you can buy fresh trout to take home. Enthusiasts with the necessary licence pay 14 to 18 euros for a day's fishing (all year except Mondays) and can keep up to 10 trout.

A pleasant walk of about one kilometre up the valley past abandoned flour mills brings you to the point where Río Frío gushes from the rock. Year round it stays at the same cool temperature.

From Riofrío it is a fast run back to Málaga, 69 kilometres along the A92, A359 and N331.

Continuing towards Granada, you sight Loja (pop. 21,000), straggling below the highway and across the Genil river. The town stands on a narrow section of the valley, a strategic spot on the Málaga-Granada route.

Successive conquerors occupied this site and the Moors knew it as Medina Lauxa, until they were ousted in 1486. Walls and towers

Prize catch for a Río Frío trout fisherman

of their fortress remain. Seven centuries ago Loja-born Ibn al-Jatib, poet, historian, traveller and Vizir at the court of Granada, claimed: "My city has a smiling face, the aspect of a charmer and of beautiful women who cure the ills of the heart."

Many of Loja's streets and historic buildings are being refurbished and several convents and churches, including 16th-century San Gabriel, built to the plans of Diego de Siloé, are worth visiting. Loja is proud of its fountains. The most notable are La Fuente de los 25 Caños (The Fountain of the 25 Spouts) and the La Fuente de los Cuatro Caños.

Near the latter, in the Plaza de Arriba, stands a statue of General Narváez, a military hero and prime minister born here. Known as El Espadón (Top Brass) de Loja, he was confronted by Rafael Pérez del Alamo, leader of a revolt of the landless, 6000 of whom occupied the town for five days in 1861.

From Loja, you can either head directly to Granada along the not-very-interesting A92 or make a detour to a particularly picturesque town. Take the N321 north. Near Ventorros de San José lies the Megalithic Necropolis of Sierra Martilla, with a series of rock tombs. Some 28 kilometres from Loja, branch east, reaching Montefrío (pop. 7500) after a further 15 kilometres.

High on a crag dominating the town is La Villa, a Renaissance church built over an Arab fortress. In the centre of town rises Encarnación church. Unusually for Andalusia, this is in the Neo-classic style to the plans of a famed architect, Ventura Rodríguez. Scores of swifts and swallows have made their nests below the vast cupola.

The locals are proud of their pork products, olive oil and a prize-winning cheese—the *queso montefriaño*. In the hunting season, partridge and rabbit are on local menus.

From Montefrío, head east on the Illora road. After four kilometres you reach the Peñas de los Gitanos necropolis, rated one of the most important archeological sites in the province. There are about 100 megalithic tombs here and Roman, Visigothic and Arab remains spread over a wooded landscape of gorges and meadows. Park your car on the right of the highway and approach on foot.

Beyond the necropolis, the Illora road curves right but you continue straight ahead for 12 kilometres on a good new road (unmarked on most maps) to Puerto López. Here you join the N342. As it begins to descend towards Granada, you catch your first glimpse of the snow-capped Sierra Nevada, floating like a mirage above the haze.

WHAT TO SEE

Málaga:

Montes de Málaga: views of Málaga and the coast.

Lagar de Torrijos, C345, km544. Ecological museum. Open usually 10am-2pm, 4-6pm, closed Mon-Wed. Call 952 04 21 00 to check times.

Loja:

Encarnación church, Gothic and neo-classic styles, on site of mosque.

San Gabriel church, magnificent facade, built 1552 to plans of Diego de Siloé.

Santa Clara, 16th-century Franciscan convent with Mudéjar panelling.

Ayuntamiento, elegant palatial residence of Narváez, his oil painting is in the council hall.

Los Infiernos, Genil river gorge with waterfalls.

Montefrío:

La Villa, Renaissance church built over an Arab fortress, renovated as an interpretation centre of Andalusia's Moorish heritage.

Encarnación church, open 10am-1pm, 7.30-8.30pm, closed Sun pm.

San Antonio church, open for mass, Wed & Sat 6pm, Sun 10am. Once part of a Franciscan convent. Plateresque facade and an 18th-century cloister.

Necropolis, Ctra de Illora, Peña de los Gitanos (4 km from Montefrío), open 9am-2pm.

WHERE TO STAY

Malaga:

Humaina, Ctra de Colmenar, Paraje el Cerrado, Málaga. Tel. 952 64 10 25. Family-run, in tranquil valley. Riding, hiking, cycling. Pool. Traditional dishes in restaurant. €€€

Ríogordo:

Hospedería Retamar, Partido Pujeo 30, Riogordo. Tel. 952 03 12 25. Farmhouse in isolated hillside setting. Excellent local food served. €€€

Old plaque at Venta de Alfarnate

Montefrío:
La Enrea, Paraje de la Enrea, s/n, Montefrío. Tel. 958 33 66 62.
Comfortable three-star hotel built in traditional style on site of an
oil mill. €€

WHERE TO EAT

Málaga:
Venta Galwey, Ctra de los Montes, km544, Málaga. Tel. 952 11 01
28. Located 19km from Málaga, one of many good-value ventas
on C345. Specialities venison, wild boar etc.

Alfarnate:
Venta de Alfarnate, Antigua Ctra Málaga-Granada. Tel. 952-75 93
88. Open 11am-7pm, July-Aug 12am-12pm. Closed Mon. Hearty
grills and stews. Book at weekends.

Riofrío:
Many restaurants compete for business, all serving trout in various
styles.
Mesón Coronichi, Avda La Paz, 23. Tel. 958 33 61 46. Closed Mon.
Recommended for kid and pork products.

MORE INFORMATION

Loja:
Centro de Interpretación Histórica, Plaza de Arriba. Tel. 958 32 15
20. Open: Mon-Fri 12am-2pm, Sat-Sun 12-2pm, 4.30-6.30pm.
Historic exhibition in 16th-century former town hall.

Montefrío:
Tourist office, Plaza de España, 1. Tel. 958 33 60 04. Open Mon-
Fri 9.30am-2pm, 4.30-6pm, Sat-Sun 9.30am-2pm.

Málaga:
Montes de Málaga nature park office, Molina Larios, 13-2º,
Málaga. Tel. 952 22 58 00.

A Poet's Journey

Patio de Los Leones, Alhambra

FEDERICO GARCÍA LORCA, ONE OF THE GREATEST SPANISH POETS AND DRAMATISTS OF RECENT TIMES, WAS PROFOUNDLY INFLUENCED BY HIS CHILDHOOD AND LIFE AS A YOUNG MAN IN GRANADA. HE HATED SOME ASPECTS OF THE CITY, BUT HE ALSO LOVED IT - "THE HOURS ARE LONGER AND SWEETER THERE THAN IN ANY OTHER SPANISH TOWN," HE ONCE COMMENTED. HE HIMSELF WAS LOVED AND HATED, AS IT TURNED OUT WHEN HE WAS KILLED AT THE START OF THE SPANISH CIVIL WAR.

AREA: In and around city of Granada
ROUTE: Granada→Fuente Vaqueros→Valderrubio→Moclín→Víznar →Granada.
DISTANCE: 100 kilometres

3 A Poet's Journey

This route takes you to Lorca's birthplace outside Granada and some of the places he frequented in the city, from where he drew inspiration for a number of his most famous works.

Head west on the Málaga and Seville road, the A329 towards Santa Fe and Granada airport. The Catholic Monarchs camped at Santa Fe with their army in 1491, when they were laying siege to Granada. A royal maid is said to have left a candle too close to a curtain in Queen Isabel's tent and flames destroyed the campground. King Fernando thereupon ordered a proper town built and Isabel chose the name, which means "holy faith". The capitulation of Granada was signed there in November, 1491. Apart from its historical significance, however, Santa Fe is an unexciting place.

Fourteen kilometres from Granada, turn right to Chauchina. Follow the signs for Fuente Vaqueros as the road zig-zags through Chauchina, a farming community with trundling tractors holding up faster traffic. Fuente Vaqueros is three kilometres from Chauchina, across the Genil river and through typical scenery in the Vega, the fertile plain which spreads out from the hills of Granada and which a Moorish historian likened to "a silver bowl filled with emeralds and precious stones".

Large plantations of poplars dot the landscape. In between them everything from maize to melons grows in the well-watered soil. Barns with openwork brick walls allow breezes to flow through and dry the harvested tobacco leaves.

Fuente Vaqueros (pop. 3700) itself is unremarkable, although Lorca recalled it lyrically - "surrounded with poplars, which laugh and sing and are palaces of birds, and elders and blackberries, which in summer give fruit that is sweet and difficult to pick".

Off the long main square, with its cafes, shady trees and an ugly modern monument to the poet, lies the Casa-Museo Federico García Lorca, where he was born. Lorca attended school in Calle Manuel de Falla, around the corner from his first home in Calle Trinidad, which has been renamed Calle Poeta García Lorca.

A guide shows visitors around Number 4, a simple, two-storey building. The carefully arranged contents include the wooden and brass bed in which Lorca was born on June 11, 1898, photographs, copies of first editions, childhood sketches and letters by the poet to Dalí's sister Ana María. The first floor, formerly a granary, has been converted into a hall where exhibitions on Lorca-related themes are held.

Fuente Vaqueros has an English connection, since it once formed part of a *latifundio* or vast estate, known as Soto de Roma. This was donated by Spain in 1813 to the Duke of Wellington in gratitude for his part in ousting Napoleon's troops from the peninsula. The Duke never bothered to visit and his descendants no longer have holdings here, although they still own the Molino del Rey estate near Illora, to the north.

Continue to neighbouring Valderrubio, some four kilometres to the northwest. When Lorca was nine, the family moved here. At that time this village bore the unfortunate name Asquerosa (meaning "disgusting"). No doubt weary of neighbours' gibes, village leaders changed the name to Valderrubio in 1943.

The Lorcas spent two to three years here before moving to Granada. Near their first house, in Calle Real, was the home of Frasquita Alba, a woman of strong character on whom Lorca based his play "The House of Bernarda Alba". For most of their stay, the family lived at Number 20 on Calle de la Iglesia.

Hot on the trail of the inspiration for some of Lorca's most famous works, we head north from Valderrubio towards Illora, turning right at a T-junction towards Zujaira and Pinos Puente. We pass through olive groves and reach the N432, the Granada-Córdoba highway. Turn right, then left on a minor road to Moclín. The road follows the Frailes river, then loops upwards to Moclín (pop. 5100), squatting on its hilltop.

Queen Isabel and King Fernando lodged at the castle here while they tightened the screws on the Kingdom of Granada. After Granada's fall in 1492, they gave Moclín a standard used in the campaign. This canvas, depicting Christ shouldering the Cross, was installed in the church and over the centuries a cult grew up around it. The Santo Cristo del Paño, as it came to be known, was credited with curative powers and, in particular, it was said to work miracles on infertile women.

Lorca heard about the Cristo and the bizarre scenes accompanying the annual pilgrimage to Moclín. This apparently sowed the seeds that led him to write the play "Yerma". You can see the famous canvas in the sanctuary inside the castle walls and, on October 5, you can witness it being carried in the romería, held every year.

From Moclín it is 36 kilometres back to Granada, taking the fastest route via Puerto López on the N432.

Within the city itself many spots recall the poet's life there. Opposite the Correos (post office) on the Puerto Real is the facade of an old building that housed El Suizo, a famous Granada cafe and meeting place. García Lorca frequently sat at one of its marble tables, joking and debating with his friends. Today a new cafe has been installed, where youngsters tuck into hamburgers and ice cream.

Not far away along the Acera del Darro, which leads to the Genil river, is the house the Lorca family first occupied in Granada. Today it is part of the Hotel Montecarlo.

From there it is a few steps to the Plaza del Campillo and a cafe now called the Chikito. It is much changed from the days in the early 1920s when it was known as the Café Alameda and a rendezvous of writers, artists, musicians, young idealists, all eager and ambitious. Here Lorca enjoyed lively conversations with composer Manuel de Falla. The two helped to organise a legendary cante jondo (flamenco-singing) festival in the Alhambra in 1922.

Lorca's friendship with Manuel de Falla undoubtedly took him to the composer's house on Antequeruela Alta, 11 (near the Alhambra Palace hotel). This is a typical Granada house, or *carmen*, with a garden. It has been converted into a museum with the original furnishings, including the composer's piano, desk and pictures.

Lorca's interest in flamenco was encouraged by his wanderings over Sacromonte and his contacts with the large community of gypsies inhabiting the caves. This helped inspire one of his most popular poetic works, "Romancero Gitano".

Another place where it is more than likely Lorca passed some idle moments is the Antigua Bodega Castañeda, on Calle Elvira, where the bull's head, the beams, the barrels and the veterans at the bar give the sensation that little has changed since its founding a hundred or so years ago.

From 1925 the Lorca family spent their summers at the Huerta de San Vicente, an enchanting old farmhouse on the Vega with views of the Alhambra. Here Lorca wrote some of his most famous works, including Blood Wedding.

To reach the Huerta, go west from Puerto Real along Recogidas street, turn right on the Camino de Ronda and then left along Virgen Blanca. The city has invaded the once-tranquil farmland. Characterless apartment blocks reach almost to the Huerta and a bypass carries heavy traffic on its western side.

But the old house survives, surrounded now by a municipal park. Granada town hall has created the Casa-Museo de Lorca there, restoring the farmhouse to its original state. The poet's bed, piano and other belongings have been donated by his family.

This was where Lorca returned to from Madrid at the start of the Spanish Civil War in 1936, ill-advisedly for he had antagonised fanatical right wingers who supported Franco's uprising.

On August 9, Lorca took refuge in the house of friends in the city. A few days later he was arrested by the Nationalist rebels, who had taken over the city, and conducted to the offices of the Civil Governor, now the Law Faculty of Granada University, on Calle Duquesa.

From here we can follow Lorca's route after it had been decided that he must die. Follow the signs on the Gran Vía and the Avenida de la Constitución that point to the Murcia road. This takes you up a steep, one-way street. At the junction at the top, where the Murcia road swings right, follow the sign to the left to La Cartuja and Alfacar.

You pass the magnificent Baroque church of La Cartuja and a rather dismal suburb of high-rise blocks. Take the road to the right to Víznar. It runs up along a ridge planted with olive trees and with fine views of the mountains, city and Vega.

The road crosses the A92 auto route and we pass through the narrow streets of Víznar (pop. 680), with its old church and archbishop's palace, and follow the road that curves around the hillside to Alfacar. Lorca and his fellow-prisoners were held in a grim, barely furnished building just outside Víznar, awaiting their execution.

From here hundreds of prisoners - nobody knows exactly how many - were taken at dawn to the nearby Barranco de Víznar, where they were shot.

Carry on along the Alfacar road. Opposite a modern block of apartments is the Lorca memorial park, opened on April 27, 1986. Inside, a granite block marks the spot where the poet is believed to have been shot. His remains were apparently buried by the olive tree standing alongside.

A brick entrance and iron gates lead to the park, surrounded by poplars and cedars and dedicated to Lorca and all victims of the Civil War. Ceramic plaques on the walls record some of the poet's verses. Weeds are sprouting in the park, the water channels are usually dry and the gates often closed.

A little beyond the park, on the left, is a pool of clear water. This is the Fuente Grande, from which water has been channelled to Granada since Arab times. Appropriately, the Moors gave it the name "Spring of Tears".

It is possible to return to Granada by continuing on this road to Alfacar. Near the old village church with its square stone tower is a bakery, recalling the fame this village has always had for the quality of its bread. From Alfacar it is eight kilometres back to the city.

Note: Aficionados of Lorca and his work can enter deeper into his world by reading Lorca's Granada: A practical guide (Faber & Faber 1992) or the Spanish version, Guía a la Granada de Federico García Lorca (Plaza & Janes 1989). This book is written by Ian Gibson, the poet's acclaimed biographer, whose painstaking investigations finally uncovered the truth about his death.

Patio de los Leones, Alhambra

García Lorca plaque, Viznar

WHAT TO SEE

Fuente Vaqueros:

Casa-Museo Federico García Lorca, Fuente Vaqueros. Tel. 958-44 64 53. Visits on the hour 10am-1pm, 6-8pm (earlier in winter). Closed Mon. Entry 1.20 euros.

Granada:

Huerta de San Vicente, Calle Virgen Blanca, 6 (off Camino de Ronda), Granada. Tel. 958 25 84 66. Open 10am-1pm, 5pm-8pm. Closed Mon. Entry 1.80 euros.

Casa-Museo Manuel de Falla, Antequeruela Alta, 11 (near Alhambra Palace hotel), Granada. The composer's home is closed while repairs are made.

Alhambra. One of Spain's top sights. Open: 8.30am-6pm (Nov-Feb), 8.30am-8pm (Mar-Oct). Entry 7.88 euros. Open some evenings. To avoid queuing and delays, buy tickets in advance via the internet: <u>www.alhambratickets.com</u>, at Banco de Bilbao y Vizcaya branches, or by calling 902 22 44 60.

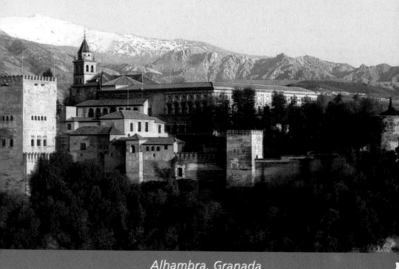

Alhambra, Granada

WHERE TO STAY

Granada:

Alhambra Palace, Peña Partida, 2. Tel: 958 22 14 68. Luxury Moorish-style hotel near Alhambra. Fine views. Less expensive than Granada's (usually fully booked) Parador. €€€€

América, Real de la Alhambra, 53. Tel: 958 22 74 71. One-star hotel within Alhambra walls. Closed Nov-Feb. €€€.

Carmen de Santa Inés, Placeta de Porras, 7, Albaicín. Tel: 958 22 63 80. Intimate three-star hotel in charming 16th-century house. €€€€.

Suecia, Huerta Los Angeles, 8 (off Calle Molinos). Tel: 958 22 50 44. Tranquil, budget two-star hostal. Parking is handy. €€

WHERE TO EAT

Granada:

Los Manueles, Zaragoza, 2. Tel: 958 22 34 13. Typical Granada dishes, traditional decor.

Mesón Antonio, Ecce Homo, 6 (near Campo de Príncipe). Tel: 958 22 95 99. Closed: Sun & July-August. Ring to enter. Intimate atmosphere. Home cooking.

Mirador de Morayma, Pianista García Carrillo, Albaicín. Tel: 958-22 82 90. Closed Sun. Well-prepared Granada dishes in fine old house.

Taberna Casa Enrique (Acera del Darro, 8) and *Antigua Bodega Castañeda* (Calle Elvira, 5). Among the oldest of many good tapa bars.

MORE INFORMATION

Granada:

Tourism office, Junta de Andalucía, Corral del Carbón, Calle Mariana Pineda, Granada. Tel: 958 22 59 90. Open 9am-7pm, Sun 10am-2pm.

Andalusia's Ice Cube

View of Sierra Nevada

ANDALUSIA'S ICE CUBE, THE SIERRA NEVADA, HAS A GRANDEUR ALL ITS OWN. FROM PARCHED, FAR-OFF OLIVE GROVES YOU CAN GLIMPSE ITS GLITTERING SNOWS AND ITS WATERS HELP TO KEEP MUCH OF THE REGION ALIVE.

AREA: Granada province
ROUTE: Granada→Sierra Nevada→Río Genil→Guéjar Sierra→Granad
DISTANCE: 80 kilometres

Despite its height above sea level, the highway to the Sierra Nevada is simple to drive as there are no really steep gradients or hair-raising bends. Costly improvements were made in the early 1990s as far as the ski resort at Pradollano, and only in winter - when all motorists are advised to carry chains - can it be difficult.

Leaving Granada on the Paseo de la Bomba, you pass in the park two yellow tramcars, recalling the days when trams rattled and rolled through the city and out to distant points in the country. They continued to run until the early 1970s.

Fill up before leaving town, as once out of Granada on this route petrol stations are few and far between. The much-improved A395 road runs along the Genil valley, passing orchards and stands of poplar trees. At Cenes de la Vega a building frenzy has transformed the village and a wall of concrete rises up the valley-side.

At Pinos Genil, the road begins to climb upwards and you glimpse a colossal wall blocking the valley, a dam creating the Embalse de Canales. There is a viewing point on the left.

Just past La Higuera hostal and restaurant, a narrow side-road to the right shins up the mountainside towards El Purche, from where there are excellent views.

You cross an old track known as the Camino de los Neveros. This was the route taken by muleteers descending from the mountains with loads of ice and snow. From Moorish times the *neveros* (from nieve, snow) earned a living bringing a breath of coolness to those *granadinos* who could afford the luxury.

Twenty-three kilometres from Granada, near the Mirador Las Víboras, on a side road to the left stands the Centro de Visitantes El Dornajo. It's worth stopping here to inform yourself on all aspects of the Sierra Nevada, including possible walks. Maps and local products, such as honey and cheese, are on sale.

Near here are a group of hotels and restaurants, including El Guerra and Santa Cruz, named after Juan José Santa Cruz, the engineer responsible for the road to the Sierra Nevada.

Below a petrol station you will see a surprisingly bright patch of emerald-green, a football ground. Retrieving a ball kicked out of play must require mountaineering skills as the pitch is perched high on the mountainside, with the village of Güéjar-Sierra visible far below.

The road climbs steadily, but without any excessive gradients, entering the upper levels of the Monachil river valley. Great ridges run upwards, planted here and there with conifers. The country is generally eroded and rounded without any Alpine-style spectacular peaks. The grey rocks definitely look more attractive under a layer of snow.

Even the snow cannot do much to soften the jarring outlines of the hotel and apartment blocks at Pradollano, the centre of the Solynieve skiing area at 2100 metres above sea level. Thirty-three kilometres from Granada, the resort underwent huge expansion for world ski championships in the 1990s.

Skiers career down more than 60 kilometres of marked runs from as high as the Veleta summit, 3398 metres above sea level. The wide, treeless slopes are recommended for beginners and intermediates. There is also cross-country skiing.

In season (December to late April), Pradollano's bars, restaurants and hotels buzz with life. If you intend skiing here, double your usual skin protection, as this is Europe's southernmost ski slope and in spring the sun shines with African intensity. Off-season, only one or two cafes and hotels are open.

Running from Granada province into Almería, the sierra was formed 20 million years ago during the Terciary folding, and glacial action has carved out 40 lagoons. To conserve the unique environment, Spain's largest National Park has been created, covering 86,000 hectares within a total protected area of 169,000 hectares.

The sierra has 14 peaks over 3000 metres. In the summer months, it is possible to climb all 14 in a tough, three-day hike and there are other fine walking opportunities. However, nobody should venture on the mountain unless they are fit and properly equipped.

Above the ski resort, the highway runs past crags known as the Peñones de San Francisco. The road zig-zags upwards to the foot of the Veleta, making it the highest road in Europe. However, you can no longer drive this route. The road is blocked to all motor traffic at the Hoya de la Mora, shortly before reaching a monument to the Virgen de las Nieves - a measure designed to protect the unique ecological balance in these mountains.

A control point has been established at the Hoya de la Mora (tel. 630 95 97 39), and a second one on the south side, at Hoya del Portillo (tel. 686 41 45 76), 11 kilometres from Capileira in the Alpujarras (see Excursion 20). Between July and September (depending on weather conditions) call these numbers to sign on for minibus trips, with interpretation service, up to higher points from where you can walk to the Veleta and Mulhacén.

If you walk from the Hoya de la Mora to the Veleta, it will take you about three hours. From the top, there are magnificent views of the mountains and possibly a glimpse of the Mediterranean and Africa. On a ridge near the ski slopes the white bowl of a radio telescope scans the heavens.

Every August 5, people of the sierras pay homage to the Virgen de las Nieves in the Romería Blanca. Her small image is carried up by torchlight from Pradollano to a lofty spot near the Veleta peak, and just after dawn a priest conducts a mass, often watched from adjacent slopes by wild goats.

A rocky track continues from the Veleta's south side to Capileira, a distance of about 25 kilometres. Initially, the scenery is bleak and with little vegetation as the route skirts a series of chilly lagoons – Aguas Verdes, Rio Seco, La Caldera – and jagged, slate-grey crags.

Because of the unique mix of high altitude and Mediterranean climate, a rich diversity of flora and fauna exists. Wild goats, rare butterflies, hawks and eagles patrol the glaciated slopes and 40 plants are unique to this area.

A path ascends the great bulk of Mulhacén, at 3482 metres the highest point on mainland Spain. At the summit there is a religious shrine, from where you gaze down on precipitous cliffs and chasms. Mulhacén gets its name from one of the last Moorish kings of Granada. Nature-lovers managed to block a Defence Ministry proposal to build a satellite-tracking station on the summit in the 1990s.

The track continues over open moorland more than 2500 metres above sea level as it follows the Piedra Blanca ridge. You glimpse Trevélez in the valley to your left. Then the route weaves downwards past grazing flocks of sheep and plantations of pines, executing a series of hairpins as it approaches Capileira.

While reasonably fit trekkers may not find this route over-demanding, don't under-estimate the effort required at this altitude. Take food and warm clothing in case you find yourselves spending the night on the mountain.

Those not looking for such an energetic hike should drive back towards Granada. You reach a junction where the main road to Pradollano and Granada curves left. Swing to the right on the original road to the sierra. It wiggles down and, shortly before rejoining the main Granada road at Mirador La Víbora, you see a sharp right turn. A signpost points to Seminario Sierra Nevada and Maitena.

This is a narrow, twisting six-kilometre road down to the Genil river. It is marked "Camino estrecho y muy peligroso" (narrow, dangerous road). However, if you drive with due precaution, there is little danger, although it should be avoided in winter and early spring when it can be icy.

In parts this route is like an English country lane. Cherry and chestnut trees flourish on the hillside, in sharp contrast to the bare slopes on the other side of the Genil valley.

You pass a religious retreat located in a large building known as the Hotel del Duque. This property, once a gambling casino, was built by the Duque de San Pedro Galatino, a colourful entrepreneur responsible for the construction of the Hotel Alhambra Palace in Granada and the city's tram services.

14 Andalusia's Ice Cube

On the last stretch, through leafy shade, a series of hairpin bends bring you to the Genil river. Immediately after crossing the river, turn sharp right through a tunnel. The signs point to Barranco San Juan and Vereda de la Estrella. A narrow, paved road follows the river for 2.3 kilometres to an information point.

Here, you can enjoy a delightful walk along La Vereda de la Estrella. The path is not difficult and takes you deep into the sierras along a narrow gorge, the breeze rustling through the trees as the river splashes along below. It takes about three hours to reach a cave known as La Cueva Secreta.

Refreshments are available at several restaurants in the Genil valley. The road follows the old track of the *tranvías* (trams), plunging through tunnels at several points. The stone structure of the Maitena station, converted into a bar and restaurant, still stands. There are roses over the doorway, flowering bushes and geraniums in profusion. You can enjoy a drink and look down on a swimming hole below.

After many curves, the village of Güéjar-Sierra (pop. 2800) appears. Flowers adorn the narrow back-streets and old men gossip around the fountain in the square, belying a turbulent past. After the 16th-century Morisco rebellion, Güéjar's inhabitants were expelled and their property shared out between 100 Christian families.

Placed under Granada's jurisdiction, the new residents kicked up a storm until Güéjar was ceded to them. One condition was that every year they donated rushes and other greenery to decorate Granada's streets for the Corpus Christi procession.

After Güéjar the road widens, passing cherry and plum orchards and climbing above the flooded valley floor. The Canales reservoir, to your left, holds the waters of the Genil between steep rock walls. Soon the road is running above the village of Pinos Genil. It meets the main Sierra Nevada highway and we turn right to return to Granada.

Note: A good map of the Sierra Nevada is published by the Instituto Geográfico Nacional on a scale of 1:50,000.

WHERE TO STAY

Sierra Nevada:

El Guerra, Ctra Sierra Nevada, km 21. Tel: 958 48 48 36. Two stars. Renovated. Pool. Restaurant. €-€€

Santa Cruz, Ctra Sierra Nevada km 23. Tel: 958 48 48 00. Three stars. Tennis, pool, sauna. €€-€€€

Pradollano Ski Resort has many hotels but most are closed outside the ski season.

Río Genil

WHERE TO EAT

Sierra Nevada:

El Desvío, Ctra de la Sierra, km 23. Tel. 958 34 01 83. Try rabbit with mushrooms.

Las Víboras, Ctra de la Sierra, km 21. Tel. 958 34 04 09. Excellent spot to eat jamón serrano, cured on the premises.

In the Genil valley:

Mesón Barranco San Juan (only weekends except July & August), *El Charcón* and the *Maitena* are among the eating places.

Mulhacen Summit

MORE INFORMATION

Las Víboras:
Centro de Visitantes El Dornajo, Las Víboras, off A395. Tel. 958 34 06 25. Open: 10am-2.30pm, 4.30-7pm.

Granada:
Centro Administrativo del Parque Nacional. Tel. 958 02 63 00.

Federación Andaluza de Montañismo, Camino de Ronda, 101, Edificio Atalaya, 1º-7G, Granada. Tel: 958 29 13 40. Information for climbers and on mountain refuges.

Sierra Nevada

Land of the Troglodytes

Cave homes at Guadix

TAKE A TRIP TO THE UNUSUAL WORLD OF THE
TROGLODYTES AND A SPLENDID MEDIEVAL CASTLE—
AND ENJOY SOME OF ANDALUSIA'S MOST MAJESTIC
MOUNTAIN SCENERY.

AREA: Granada province
ROUTE: Granada→Purullena→Guadix→Lacalahorra→Granada
DISTANCE: 160km

From Granada, the A92 heads eastwards towards Guadix and Murcia. You climb the Puerto de la Mora, altitude 1,390 metres. It is wild country, with large tracts of pine forest and lumpy hills that rise towards the snowy heights of the Sierra Nevada.

When you approach Purullena, bypassed by the A92, the terrain changes into strange eroded shapes. The hills are honeycombed with caves, each with a whitewashed facade and a whitewashed chimney sticking out of the hillside above. A television antenna is usually attached to the chimney. You expect a Hobbit or a talkative gnome to pop out his head at any moment.

Thousands of people inhabit man-made caves in this area of Granada province. Most of the troglodytes are ordinary working-class Spaniards and extremely cave-proud. Inside, these dwellings – many with all mod cons – are whitewashed and kept as clean as any house. The temperature remains a steady 18 degrees summer or winter. When there are additions to a family, it is a simple matter to hack out another room.

Because the hills are of hard, compacted clay – part of the Guadix-Baza post-pliocene deposit if you want to get technical – they are easy to excavate and remain impermeable to rain. Just back from the highway through Purullena, a hillock hollowed out like a Gruyere cheese was until recently a disco. Once this two-storey cave was an inn welcoming weary muleteers.

Many Moriscos (Moorish converts to Christianity) are believed to have moved underground in the 17th century to escape Felipe 11's persecution. Purullena's main street is lined with shops selling a vast array of pottery, though almost all of it is imported from other regions. The area is renowned for its luscious peaches. Try some if they are in season.

Carry on to Guadix (pop. 20,000), a town famous in ancient times for its silver, iron and copper riches. The Carthaginian general Hannibal took a local princess as his concubine and Roman Emperor Augustus founded a colony here to guard an important cross roads on the route from Cartago to Nova Hispalis. Guadix inhabitants are known as "*accitanos*", from Acci, the ancient name of the settlement.

It is not Andalusia's most dynamic town but it does have some impressive monuments, such as the Arab fortress and the Mudéjar Santiago church. There is a large troglodyte quarter, known variously as the Barrio de Santiago and Ermita Nueva. One or two caves are available for rent.

One of the best-known pieces of Spanish music has connections with Guadix. "The Three-Cornered Hat", a ballet for which Manuel de Falla composed the music, was based on a short story by Pedro Antonio Alarcón, born here.

Heading southeast towards the Almería highway, after one kilometre turn right to reach, after 12 kilometres, Jeres del Marquesado (also spelled "Jérez"), a delightful old village. An imposing iron-studded door gives access to the 16th-century Jeres church, which features Moorish-style brickwork, massive pillars, and a beautiful altarpiece.

Here you are on one of the highest plateaus in Spain, the Marquesado de Zenete, more than 1000 metres above sea level. A pleasant country road leads to Lacalahorra. You pass Alquife, where iron was formerly mined. A British company has announced plans to install a high-tech park and a tourist resort here, but don't hold your breath.

Lacalahorra is dominated by a unique Italian Renaissance palace, concealed inside grim castle walls. You cannot miss the rectangular castle, with its circular towers, standing proudly austere atop a hillock.

The castle is open on Wednesdays, although you may be able to gain access on other days if you can find the guardian, Antonino Tribaldoz, who was actually born in the castle. The proud structure was built by Rodrigo de Mendoza, son of Cardinal Mendoza, between 1509 and 1512, with the aid of Italian craftsmen. Rodrigo, Marquis of Zenete, was given this area, with its six villages, by the Catholic Monarchs.

The patio is graced by columns and a staircase of Carrara marble and there are some fine coffered ceilings in bedrooms. Note a grim narrow dungeon slotted between the walls – this was for female prisoners.

South of the village, the A337 scales the 2000-metre Puerto de la Ragua to enter the Alpujarras region, on the south side of the Sierra Nevada. Ice and snow can make this pass hazardous. In winter, when it rains in Guadix it is probably snowing higher up, so inquire about conditions from the Civil Guard. A timber refuge and information point at the top, next to a picnic area, aim to provide facilities for cross-country skiing.

From Lacalahorra you can return direct to Granada along the A92 or branch off at Purullena to explore some more back roads. A road runs south from Purullena into the foothills of the Sierra Nevada. If you take a left fork, a well-watered valley leads to hamlets like Polícar and Lugros, remote from everyday life, with the massive mountain barrier soaring to their rear.

Taking the right fork brings you back to Granada by a tortuous route but one offering magnificent mountain views. You pass Graena, a small spa (open June-October, tel. 958 66 03 50) offering solace for the ailing and the stressed-out. Rheumatism and arthritis are among the complaints that the waters, issuing from the rock at 44 degrees C, are claimed to help.

From there a narrow road wanders over the hills, skirting the Quéntar reservoir, a startling emerald green below sheer ochre cliffs. There are frequent warnings advising cyclists that the road is narrow and dangerous. You pass the small villages of Quéntar and Dúdar, before reaching Cenes de la Vega on the Genil valley and the outskirts of Granada.

WHERE TO STAY

Guadix:

Hotel Comercio, Mira de Amezcua, 3, Guadix. Tel: 958 66 05 00. Three-star hotel with restaurant. €€

Cuevas Pedro Antonio de Alarcón, Bda. San Torcuato, s/n, Guadix. Tel: 958 66 49 86. Caves refurbished as apartments, kitchen included. €€

Reina Isabel, 30km north of Guadix at Baños de Alicún de las Torres, tel: 958 69 40 22. Two-star hotel and spa. Hot spring. Steam-baths, saunas and massage. Open April-November.

Lacalahorra:

Hostal Labella, Crta de Aldeire, 1. Tel 958 67 70 00. Pleasantly rustic, recently constructed. 12 rooms. €

WHERE TO EAT

Guadix:

Hotel Comercio. Traditional local dishes such as lamb in honey with raisins and pine nuts.

Lacalahorra:

Hostal Labella. No-frills, hearty local dishes.

Lacalahorra castle with Sierra Nevada at rear

Cascamorras Oil Festival

WHAT TO SEE

Guadix:

Municipal Cueva-Museo (museum in a cave), Barrio Ermita Nueva. Open Mon-Fri, 10am-2pm, 4-6pm. Sat-Sun 10am-2pm. Closed Mon.

Cathedral museum. Open Mon-Sat 11am-1pm, 4-6pm. Closed Sun. Impressive Baroque-Renaissance, partly designed by Diego de Siloé; Alcazaba (Arab fortress) open Mon-Sat 10am-2pm. Closed Sunday.

Alcazaba Cave Museum open 10am-2pm, 4.30-8.30pm.

Lacalahorra:

Lacalahorra Castle, open Wednesdays, 10am-1pm, 4-6pm.

MORE INFORMATION

Guadix:

Tourist office, Avda Mariana Pineda, s/n (also known as Ctra de Granada). Tel: 958 66 26 65. Open Mon-Fri 9am-2pm.

Granada:

Junta de Andalucía information office, Corral del Carbón, Granada, Tel. 958 22 10 22/59 60.

Rescuing the Virgin

An interesting tour extension from Guadix takes you 42 kilometres east along the A92 through austere, steppe-like country to Baza. The first week of every September Guadix despatches a volunteer, known as El Cascamorras, to Baza to bring back a coveted image of the Virgin from the Franciscan convent of La Merced. But the youths of Baza, in a riotous fiesta, drench him with dirty oil and send him back empty-handed.

Ancient cultures existed around Baza and in 1971 a large seated figure, believed to be a 2400-year-old Iberian goddess, was discovered in a necropolis. The Dama de Baza can be seen in the Museo Arqueológico in Madrid, but Baza has a copy in its museum.

Baza (Basti to the Romans) has some handsome buildings, including the Gothic Colegiata de Santa María, with an entrance attributed to Diego de Siloé and a fine tower built in 1764, and the Mudéjar-style Palacio de los Enriquez. In the old Jewish quarter are some 10th century Arab baths.

Or for something a little different, head for Galera, 42 kilometres to the northeast, via N342 and the C3329. Here you can spend the night in a cave-home. Abandoned hillside caves have been tastefully converted and furnished, with bathrooms and fully-equipped kitchens, by an enterprising local couple.

Galera is a strange little place, which experiences extremes of heat and cold. It produces its own wine, using methods long abandoned elsewhere. And it has another point of interest - more than 130 tombs and an alabaster image of a fertility goddess have been discovered in the Tutugi necropolis, from the pre-Christian era.

Accommodation recommended:

In Baza - *Robemar* (Ctra de Murcia, km175, Baza. Tel. 958-86 07 04. €), comfortable two-star hotel.

In Galera - *Casas-Cueva* (Granada, 99. Tel. 958-73 90 68. €€), Miguel and Dolores Rodríguez offer cave apartments.

A handy Galera restaurant serving typical dishes and local wine is *Méson La Zalona*, Avda Nicasio Tomas, 15. Tel: 958 73 90 32.

To the Moors'
Last Stronghold

The snowy heights of Sierra Nevada rise above the Alpujarras

WHEN THE CATHOLIC KINGS CONQUERED THE KINGDOM OF GRANADA IN 1492, MANY MOORS FLED TO THE ALPUJARRAS, THE PRECIPITOUS BUT WELL-WATERED SOUTHERN SLOPES OF THE SIERRA NEVADA. TODAY THIS SCENIC AREA IS BEING INVADED BY NEW SETTLERS LOOKING FOR A SIMPLER LIFE-STYLE.

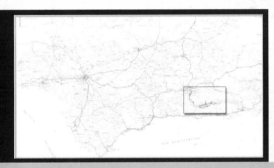

AREA: Granada province
ROUTE: Granada→Lanjarón→Orgiva→Pampaneira→Yegen→Laujar→Cádiar→Torvizcón→Granada
DISTANCE: 280km

To the Moors' Last Stronghold

The Alpujarras is a great area for walking, riding and mountain biking and this journey takes you through its heart.

Head south on the N323 from Granada, turning left on the A348 to Lanjarón, 46 kilometres from the provincial capital. Lanjarón (pop. 4200), is famed for its waters. Scores of snow-fed springs bubble from the mountain, each with particular curative properties.

Millions of litres of water are distributed throughout Spain and thousands of visitors arrive to take, under medical supervision, bubble baths, water massages and other treatment to improve their health. For information, contact the Balneario (Avenida de Andalucía, 1. Tel: 958 77 01 37). The spa is open between March and December.

Ten kilometres further along the A348, at the cross-roads known as El Empalme, turn right to Orgiva (pop. 5000), the main administrative centre of the Alpujarras.

Only recently have better communications brought the region into closer contact with the outside world. The Alpujarras now attracts expatriates of all nationalities, from New Agers and hippies to those just fleeing the rat race. A fair cross-section emerge from their hideaways to attend Orgiva's Thursday morning market. You'll see adverts for everything from organic food to astrology and massages.

The clock on the 16th-century church appears to have stopped. The previous time piece, stored in one of the twin towers, achieved notoriety. The town hall bought it in 1887 but neglected to pay for it. The Ayuntamiento finally coughed up the 4000 pesetas it owed - to the clockmaker's 83-year-old grandson 102 years later.

North of Orgiva, the GR421 corkscrews up towards the Poqueira valley. In spring the white of the almond trees matches the snow on the high peaks. In early summer you may catch sight of farmers threshing in the centuries-old way with a mule pacing around a circular, stone threshing ground.

The splashes of white on distant hillsides are villages founded centuries ago under Moorish rule. The dwellings are similar in style to those of the Berbers in North Africa, with stone walls and flat roofs of slate and rubble.

The Moors instituted ingenious irrigation systems to use the abundant water and grow all manner of fruit and crops. Silk weaving was an important industry. But though they converted to Christianity they suffered continual persecution and finally rose in rebellion under Aben Humeya in 1568. After a brutal war the Moriscos, as converts were known, were ejected from their lands.

Opposite a small chapel en route to Pampaneira, a road (marked "Ruta Pintoresca") to the left leads to a loftily situated meditation centre, O Sel Ling (Place of Clear Light), given its name by the Dalai Lama when he visited.

Soon you reach Pampaneira, first village of the picturesque Poqueira valley. Three villages are slotted into the valley sides, Pampaneira (pop. 364), Bubión (pop. 335) and at the top Capileira (pop. 605), just below the snowline.

Pampaneira, closed to traffic but with a large car park at the entrance, has several restaurants around its square. It can get crowded at weekends. Handmade rugs and blankets in traditional Alpujarras style are on sale in many craft shops.

All three villages have restaurants offering typical hearty country food at budget prices. Pork, ham and blood sausage, specialities in the Alpujarras, feature in the belly-filling plato alpujarreño. Vino de la Contraviesa is served in pitchers. Pink and potent, it comes from the Contraviesa range between the Guadalfeo valley and the Mediterranean.

Pampaneira has an information office for the Sierra Nevada National Park. You can no longer drive Europe's highest road to the ski resort on the north side, but there are abundant walking possibilities. A control point has been established at Hoya del Portillo (tel. 686 41 45 76), 11 kilometres from Capileira, and another on the north side at the Hoya de la Mora (tel. 630 95 97 39). Between June and

September, call these numbers to sign on for minibus trips, with interpretation service, up the mountain to points where you can hike to the Mulhacén and the Veleta (see Excursion 14).

Facilities are available for horse treks, mountain biking, and paragliding. Rafael Belmonte in Bubión (Cabalgar-Rutas Alternativas, tel/fax 958 76 31 35) runs horse-riding trips lasting a few hours or up to nine days. He can also help out with information on local accommodation.

As you continue east along GR421, you pass fields teetering on the edges of dark ravines and groves of chestnut, oak and walnut trees. Between Pitres and Pórtugos stands the Virgen de las Angustias chapel (you can catch a glimpse of her through the grill in the door). Below it is Fuente Agria. Visitors come specially to fill containers with the naturally carbonated water, rich in iron, gushing from six spouts. Across the road is a shaded picnic spot, with a kiosk selling drinks.

Meditation Centre above the Poqueira Valley

Pinned to the mountainside, Trevélez (pop. 800), claims (at 1476 metres) to be Spain's highest village. In airy sheds, thousands of hams are cured here in the shadow of the peninsula's highest peak, Mulhacen (3478 metres).

Cafes and pensions congregate around the village's lower quarter, blighted by modern construction. More tranquil and much prettier is the Barrio Alto, a labyrinth of narrow winding streets.

Legends are legion in this area. Buried near Trevélez is the treasure of the last Moorish king, Aben Humeya. The little village of Juviles also has its treasure. Somewhere nearby, three black diamonds were concealed in a secret palace by Muley Hacen, Moorish ruler of Granada. Anybody discovering these diamonds is destined to be crowned King of Granada.

You reach the A348, which wriggles along to Yegen, lying below the road. Surrounded by fields of maize and peppers and shady apricot trees, this hamlet achieved fame because the English writer Gerald Brenan once lived there. He arrived on foot - there were no roads - in 1920 and rented a house for 120 pesetas a year. Visiting friends from London's effete Bloomsbury Set were stunned by the primitive conditions. He vividly recounted his experiences in South From Granada. A plaque marks La Casa del Inglés.

Further east lies Válor (pop. 1100), said to be the birthplace of Aben Humeya. Every year during the mid-September fiesta, the villagers stage an uproarious Moriscos v Christians battle in the main square to a thunder of shotguns. The play dates from the early 17th century.

After Válor a road to the left, the A337, twists upwards to the lofty La Ragua pass and down to Guadix. This route can be icy in winter. Next stop on the A348 is the market town of Ugíjar (pop. 3100) in a fertile valley. Continuing east, you soon enter the bleaker scenery of arid Almeria province.

A good overnight halt is Laujar de Andarax (pop. 1900), a green oasis in the Andarax valley with the treeless Sierra de Gador rising beyond. Stop at the Plaza Mayor and refresh yourself at the

Shepherd and flock above Capileira

fountain. The town's water was eulogised by Francisco Villaespesa, a native son who achieved fame as a poet and dramatist. Equally worth sampling is the local wine.

The 16th-century parish church, La Encarnación, has an ornate, gilded reredos. To the left of the town hall, General Mola street leads towards El Nacimiento (the spring) - a pleasant picnic spot in years of good rain.

Aben Humeya was murdered in Laujar, not too long after he was crowned King of the Moriscos under an olive tree in Cádiar. This small market town—a fountain flows with wine at the October fiesta—lies on the return journey to Granada. The fastest way back is along the much-improved A348, which follows the south side of the Guadalfeo valley from Cádiar to Orgiva and Lanjarón.

If you have time, make a splendid detour along the A345, which branches left just outside Cádiar, then the GR443. This route runs along the top of the austere Sierra de la Contraviesa. On one side you have dazzling views of the white-capped Sierra Nevada and on the other of the azure Mediterranean.

WHAT TO SEE

Alpujarras:
Snow-capped peaks. Berber-style houses.

Capileira:
Pedro Antonio de Alarcón Museum, Local artefacts displayed in a typical Alpujarras house. Open 11.30am-2.30pm, closed Mon.

WHERE TO STAY

Bubion:
Villa Turística, Barrio Alto. Tel: 958 76 31 11. Built in traditional style, each unit has kitchen facilities and provision for a log fire. Reserve for holiday periods and weekends. €€€

Busquístar:
Alcazaba de Busquístar, Ctra Orgiva-Laujar, km 37 (4km from Trevélez). Tel. 958 85 86 87. Three-star hotel in traditional Alpujarras style. Heated pool, squash court, restaurant. €€-€€€

Weaver, Válor

Cádiar:
Alquería de Morayma, A348 Cadiar-Torvizcón. Tel. 958 34 32 21. Old farmhouse attractively adapted with traditional furnishings. €€

Orgiva:
Hotel Taray, Ctra Tablate-Albuñol km 18.5. Tel. 958 78 45 25. Three-star hotel amid 15,000 sq. m. garden. Restaurant, pool, riding facilities. €€

Trevélez:
La Fragua, San Antonio, 4. Tel. 958 85 86 26. One-star hotel in barrio alto. Fine views. Heating. €

Ugíjar:
Hostal Vidaña, Carretera de Almería s/n. Tel: 958 76 70 10. Plain but comfortable rooms. A reasonable restaurant. €

Laujar de Andarax:
Villa Turística, Tel: 950 51 30 27, Fax 950 51 35 54. Extensive grounds, panoramic views, swimming pool, tennis. €€€

Hostal Fernández, General Mola, 4, Tel. 950 11 31 28. Comfortable basic accommodation. €

WHERE TO EAT

Bubión:
La Artesa, Calle Carretera. Tel. 958 76 30 82. Alpujarras dishes served in rustic dining room or on the terrace. Closed Mon.

Laujar de Andarax:
Villa Turística, local specialities.

Hostal Fernández, proprietor Carmela serves good-value meals.

Nuevo Andarax, pleasant restaurant overlooking the valley.

Trevélez:
La Fragua, near the hotel. Excellent value. Local ham & wine. Kid with garlic.

Válor:

Aben Humeya, Los Bolos, s/n. Tel. 958 85 18 10. Game dishes, stews, Moorish influences.

MORE INFORMATION

Pampaneira:

Sierra Nevada National Park, Information on hiking, climbing, guide service. Nevadensis, Centro de Información, Tel 958 76 31 27. (See also Excursion number 14).

Granada:

Tourism office, Corral del Carbón, Calle Mariana Pineda. Tel: 958 22 59 90. Open 9am-7pm, Sun 10am-2pm.

Berber-style rooftops at Bubión

Snorkelling Heaven

Seascape at La Isleta del Moro

CLIFFS PLUNGING INTO CLEAR BLUE WATERS, LONELY BEACHES, DESERT LANDSCAPES . . . THESE ARE TO BE FOUND WITHIN EASY REACH OF THE CITY OF ALMERÍA. NOT SURPRISINGLY, THE AREA'S DRAMATIC SCENERY HAS FIGURED IN A NUMBER OF FILMS. THIS ROUTE TAKES YOU TO THE CABO DE GATA-NÍJAR NATURE PARK AND ALONG A STILL-UNTAMED COAST WHERE TARMAC OCCASIONALLY GIVES WAY TO DIRT.

AREA: coast of Almeria province
ROUTE: Almería→Cabo de Gata→San José→Las Negras→Carboneras →Almería
DISTANCE: 170km

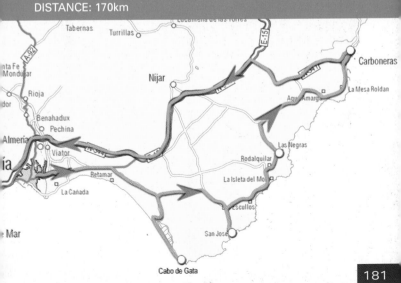

From Almería, the provincial capital, follow the signs for the airport and Cabo de Gata. The city's suburbs look more like Casablanca than a part of Spain. Fourteen kilometres out, branch right towards the sea and Retamar, then left to Cabo de Gata. On your left, amid flat scrubby country, you pass a huge greenhouse. Vast areas of the Almería desert are covered with plastic under which fruit and vegetables grown for export flourish.

You enter the Parque Natural Cabo de Gata-Níjar. It covers 34,000 hectares and includes a stretch of seabed about two kilometres wide.

Thousands of birds flying between Europe and Africa touch down amid the dunes, saltpans, and thorny jujube trees between San Miguel beach and the cape. Among the 170 bird species recorded in the park are flamingoes, Dupont's larks, griffon vultures and avocets.

Drop in at the park information centre, Las Amoladeras, where an exhibition explains the history and physical make-up of the area, with occasional video shows. Craftwork, oil and wine are on sale.

The fishing hamlet of Cabo de Gata - once dirt-poor and down-at-heel - has reinvented itself as a holiday resort. New buildings have sprung up, the roads have been paved and a posh promenade runs along the beach. Drive on along the coast and you will pass desolate salt flats and dazzling piles of salt.

The road climbs up towards the Cabo de Gata itself. At the tip of the rocky headland stands a lighthouse marking the end of the cape, near the Arrecife de las Sirenas (Sirens' Reef).

Northeast of here the track is closed to traffic. Energetic types can walk along the coast to San José through rugged country with no sign of human habitation. Not advisable in high summer as there is no shade.

Only lizards, cactus and esparto grass can scrape a living here. Ancient volcanic action has created a tortuous landscape of lava columns and craters. Steep cliffs plunge into the foaming sea and from secluded beaches divers and snorkellers launch themselves into the transparent waters. Attempts are being made to re-introduce the monk seal, which died out in the 1970s.

After trudging across a dusty plain dotted with cactus, which runs inland from the long beach of Los Genoveses, hikers hit tarmac again at San José, a small, but fast-growing, resort with a 200-berth pleasure port. Sea trips are possible from here and you can explore the park by four-wheel drive.

To reach San José by road from Cabo de Gata, retrace your route and turn right to pass by Ruescas. When you reach El Pozo de los Frailes, just inland from San José, look to the right where you see a large wooden wheel fitted with earthenware jars. This apparatus was used to crank up water from a well until the 1980s, a method unchanged since Roman times. It has been restored and forms part of an information point for the nature park.

North of El Pozo, turn towards Rodalquilar to follow the coast. Eroded hills, old windmills and cactus border the road as it winds down to lonely Los Escullos, guarded by an old fort. There are a camp ground and hotel.

Just beyond, rocks like stranded whales jut out into the sea by the primitive fishing hamlet of La Isleta del Moro. There's an end-of-the-world feeling about this place, with its fish drying in the sun and women pounding clothing at a communal wash house. Fresh fish is on the menu at the Hostal Isleta right by the water.

From here the road climbs steeply upwards. Stop at the Mirador de la Amatista to enjoy the fine views along the coast. Then continue to Rodalquilar. Abandoned when the local gold mine proved unviable, this village is being transformed into a service centre for the park.

Bypassing the village, you will see a track to the right to El Playazo. It leads to a fine beach, dominated by San Ramón castle and a backdrop of mighty cliffs. This wild area has, miraculously, not been marred by runaway development and camping is banned.

A little further on, you reach a T-junction. Turn right to reach Las Negras, with its cluster of houses (some for rent), fishing boats and gravel beach.

Turn left to go to Fernán Pérez. Entering this village, look for a right turn to Agua Amarga - it's easily missed. The road quickly becomes dirt, but it is in good condition and after nine kilometres joins a paved road to Agua Amarga.

This village on a beautiful bay, with a sandy beach and good snorkelling off the rocks, is expanding fast. Flats are available for rent and several new hotels have been built, though their prices suggest Agua Amarga has inflated views about itself.

Until recently Agua Amarga was virtually isolated, but now an excellent road scales the hills to the north. A side road leads to the Roldán lighthouse, which looks down on a cormorants' fishing area and Punta de los Muertos (Dead Man's Point), where the bodies of shipwrecked sailors were sometimes washed ashore.

The first sight of Carboneras, eight kilometres from Agua Amarga, comes as a shock. The Philistines have been at work, with their usual shortsighted ideas of "progress". A massive cement works and a power station have been built slap on the beach, with a port to serve them.

Fortunately it is a long beach and the far end is agreeable enough. The Hotel El Dorado holds reminders of Almería's Hollywood connections - the former owner, Eddie Fowlie, is an English film set decorator and location researcher and numerous films have been made in the province. You may have glimpsed the hotel's ornate front door in "Nicholas and Alexandra". The phone booth and the statues on the stairs figured in "Dr Zhivago" and elegant tasselled chairs about the hotel were props in "The Three Musketeers".

In "Lawrence of Arabia", the flat roofs of Carboneras doubled for Aqaba on the Red Sea. Scenes in "El Cid", "The Hill" and "King of Kings", not to mention countless Spaghetti Westerns (see Excursion 18), were also filmed in Almería.

Carboneras (pop. 6000) has spruced itself up considerably in recent years, although eating possibilities are still limited. Bars offer reasonable tapas, however. You will find several along the pleasant promenade.

A detour to the north will bring you to Mojácar, a mirage of white cubes, now an international resort. The coast road imitates a mountain goat as it skips along the cliff-tops, with the Sierra Cabrera rearing to the left. After 22 kilometres you reach Mojácar. According to local legend, Walt Disney was born here, a claim that baffles his relatives in the USA.

Escaping from the world of illusion, we head inland from Carboneras. The easy route is via the N341, which joins the N344 at Venta del Pobre after 19 kilometres. More adventurous types can drive up the AL101, turning right after five kilometres to El Saltador Bajo. It's easy to get lost on these side-roads - make sure you have plenty of fuel and water before hitting the wilderness.

The road runs through true desert country, cactus-dotted and unpopulated, to La Cueva del Pájaro, a huddle of houses below a hill honeycombed with caves. Entering La Cueva, look for a track to the left across the dusty river bed. It reverts to a paved surface that leads to Gafares. At a T-junction turn to the right. There are no signs to help, but eventually you should hit the AL140 and the N344. A left turn brings you swiftly back to Almería.

Ancient well at El Pozo de los Frailes   *Camping, Almería*

WHERE TO STAY

San José:

Don Ignacio, Paseo Marítimo. Tel: 950 61 10 80. Dazzling white seafront four-star hotel opened 2001, airconditioning, restaurant. €€€€

Cortijo El Sotillo, Ctra entrada a San José, tel: 950 61 11 00. Four-star hotel created around an old farmhouse. Tennis, horse-riding. €€€

Las Gaviotas, Calle Córdoba, s/n. Tel: 950 38 00 10. Well appointed two-star hostal. €€

Agua Amarga:

El Family, Calle La Lomilla. Tel: 950 13 80 14. Small French-run hostal. Pool. €€

Carboneras:

El Dorado, Camino Viejo de Garrucha, 24. Tel: 950-45 40 50, fax: 950 13 01 02. Two-star hotel, renovated. Pool. €€€

WHERE TO EAT

Agua Amarga:

Hostal Family. French-influenced cuisine with hearty helpings.

Cabo de Gata:

Mediterráneo, Calle La Iglesia, 2. Tel: 950 37 11 37. On the seafront. Fresh seafood is the speciality.

Garrucha:

El Almejero, Explanada del Puerto. Tel. 950 46 04 05. Fresh seafood - the shrimps are renowned.

San José:

Cortijo El Sotillo, traditional regional dishes.

MORE INFORMATION

Almería:

Tourist office, Parque Nicolás Salmerón, esq. Martínez Campos. Tel: 950 27 43 55. Open Mon-Fri 9am-7pm, Sat-Sun 10am-2pm.

San José:
Tourist office, Plaza Génova, s/n,. Tel: 950 38 02 99.
Open 10am-2pm, 5-8pm. Closed Sun pm.

Cabo de Gata:
Nature Park - Visitors' Centre Las Amoladeras, Cabo de Gata road,
Tel. 950 16 04 35. Open: 10am-3pm. Closed: Mon.

Rodalquilar:
Information point, Tel. 950 38 98 20. Open daily June-Sept,
Fri-Sun rest of year. Exhibition on gold mining, coastal geology.

Land of the Indalo

To explore more of eastern Almería, head north to
Vélez Rubio and Vélez Blanco (104 kilometres from
Carboneras, via Vera and the N340 and A327).

Vélez Blanco is dominated by an impressive castle
constructed in 1505 by the first Marqués de Los Vélez.
The splendid Renaissance interior was sold and
removed to New York's Metropolitan Museum early
this century. Just outside the village is Cueva de los
Letreros, sheltering prehistoric paintings. One image
depicts the Indalo, a figure holding aloft an arc, thought
to be a deity with magical powers and now used as a
symbol of Almería.

Close by lies the Sierra de María nature park covering
19,500 hectares. It's a stark, rugged area of pine forests
and sheer rock walls rising over 2000 metres. Wild boar
and golden eagles are among the wild life. Caves with
prehistoric paintings await exploration.

Accommodation includes: in Vélez Blanco, Hostal La
Sociedad (Corredera, 14. Tel. 950 41 50 27 €), simple
but immaculate, and Casa de los Arcos (San Francisco,
2. Tel: 950 61 48 05. €€), three-star hotel in renovated
old mansion. In Sierra de María nature reserve is the
comfortable two-star hotel Sierramaría (Paraje la
Moratilla, s/n, María. Tel: 950 41 71 26. €€).

Spain's Wild West

Desert terrain near Tabernas

IF YOU EVER FANCIED YOURSELF A LEE VAN CLEEF OR CLINT EASTWOOD PACING CREAKING SIDEWALKS, PUSHING OPEN BATWING DOORS AND SHOOTING IT OUT WITH A BUNCH OF DESPERADOES, THIS COULD BE THE TRIP FOR YOU. YOU TRAVEL TO THE BLEAKLY SPECTACULAR LAND OF SPAGHETTI WESTERNS AND TO A TOWN WHERE A VIOLENT REAL-LIFE DRAMA—LATER IMMORTALISED ON STAGE—WAS ONCE PLAYED OUT.

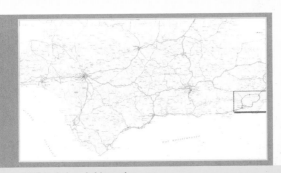

AREA: inland Almería
ROUTE: Almería→Los Millares→Tabernas→Sorbas→Nijar→Almería
ROUND TRIP: 130km

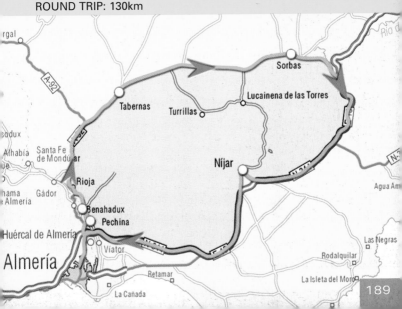

Drive north from Almería on the main Granada highway, the A92. At first it follows the Andarax valley, green with palms and citrus orchards between bare ochre hills. Two interesting detours are possible.

Detour Number One takes you to hot springs and remains of Roman baths. Turn right about 10 kilometres out of Almería, following signs for El Chuche and Pechina, then for the Balneario de Sierra Alhamilla. In the heart of a desert landscape you encounter an oasis where water gushes from the rock at 58 degrees C.

You can enjoy bubble baths and mud baths at the Balneario, a hotel with modern spa facilities. Two hundred years ago the Bishop of Almería constructed a spa here, following in the steps of Iberians, Romans and Moors. The old-style building, with its arches and tile work, has been restored and treatment is offered for rheumatism, nervous complaints, allergies, digestion, obesity and other problems.

Detour Number Two to an ancient necropolis starts further along the A92, at Benahadux. Branch left on the A348 to Alhama de Almería. After climbing beyond Gador you will see signs to the Necrópolis de Los Millares and Santa Fe de Mondújar.

A guardian is on duty (except Mondays) in a lone white building, the reception centre for Los Millares, a significant relic of human endeavour dating back more than 4000 years. He will open a gate to allow you to drive along a rocky track to the lonely site. On this arid bluff overlooking the lush Andarax valley, a community of some 2000 people flourished in the Copper and Bronze Ages. Remains of houses, workshops, mills, defensive walls, and a hundred or so tombs have been uncovered. Exploration continues.

Returning to the A92, you cross the Andarax riverbed and enter the badlands. The resemblance to Arizona and other desert regions attracted film makers here during the 1960s. Local gypsies played Indians and Mexicans and did horse-riding stunts in the Spaghetti Westerns. Movies, television productions and advertising spots are still often filmed in this area.

Twelve kilometres north of Benahadux, amid increasingly arid, harshly-scoured terrain, there is a major junction where the newly constructed A92 highway to Guadix and Granada splits from the Murcia road. Take the Guadix road and soon a track leads right, to the ranch built by Sergio Leone when he was directing such films as "The Good, the Bad and the Ugly" and "For a Fistful of Dollars". Deeper into the rocky, cactus-dotted desert stands a grim, high-walled fort, used in many a celluloid epic

However, now there's a charge for admission as this area has been converted into Western Leone - Poblado del Oeste. The attractions include a Wild West show, horses for hire, a restaurant, saloon and souvenir shop.

Double back to the road junction and turn left on the A370 over a bridge towards Tabernas and Murcia. Soon you see signs on the right for another Wild West town, Mini Hollywood. More than 100 films were made on this dusty replica of a Western town, complete with saloons, hardware stores, saddleries and a wide main street just made for High Noon encounters.

The owners have really gone to town, jazzing up the old film set and adding a zoo with more than 150 species on show. Can-Can girls whirl in The Yellow Rose saloon and "cowboys" stage shootouts. A shooting range, a movie museum, a mini-train and the chance to dress up as Daniel Boone or Calamity Jane are among the attractions.

Those with good nerves and a head for heights can make an interesting detour by following the track that runs up the mountain to the rear of Mini Hollywood. A sign warns "Route cut by chain at 300 metres". However, the chain is rarely in position and you zig-zag up a very narrow, badly paved road to the heights of the Sierra de Alhamilla, with amazing vistas of heat-hazed desert.

After 12 kilometres you reach a cluster of antennas on top of the ridge at a height of some 1300 metres. Here the road reverts to dirt and follows the ridge amid pine forest. The views are stunning. To the north lie the bleak eroded gullies and hills around Tabernas; to the south lie the Campo de Níjar and the glittering Mediterranean.

Stunt man in Spain's Wild West   *Sorbas Potter*

After nine kilometres you reach a peak topped by more antennas, for telephone and aircraft communication. Follow the paved road, which swoops down to the village of Turrillas to join the main excursion route.

If you prefer to stick to the A370, continue towards Tabernas and another example of Spaghetti Western memorabilia. Look for Texas Hollywood. A track dips into the Rambla de Tabernas, a dry river bed, then climbs to Texas. This features a Western township, a Mexican village, Indian tepees, horses, ponies and camels.

A bypass runs around the nondescript village of Tabernas and its restored castle atop a hill. In the summer months Tabernas opens its municipal swimming pool, a handy spot to escape the heat. Three kilometres beyond, a side-road to the left leads to the Plataforma Solar de Almería, a solar energy research centre.

Five kilometres from the A370, a tower juts up from the scrubby plain. Near it hundreds of heliostats (large mirrors) bounce the sun's rays into receptors, creating solar energy. You can visit the Plataforma Solar research station.

Good eating places are few and far between on this route, so it may be as well to bring a picnic with you. Between Tabernas and

Las Millares Prehistoric Village

Los Yesos there are a number of truck stops, where you can get basic meals and refreshment.

The road flattens out after Tabernas. Turn right to visit Turrillas. A narrow switchback road with spectacular views brings you to this sleepy little village pegged to the side of the Sierra de Alhamilla at 850 metres. Good water accounts for this spot being inhabited since early times. You can get good-value meals in the only bar in town, just below the church.

From Turrillas another narrow road - no safety barriers - winds east to Lucainena de las Torres, where you turn left to rejoin the A370. Just before Lucainena, stands a row of crumbling blast furnaces, monuments to past industry.

Turn east on the A370 and within nine kilometres you are in Sorbas, spectacularly situated on a bend of the Río Aguas, its houses teetering nervously on the chasm's edge. Sorbas is famed for its potters, whom you will find working away in the lower part of the village. You can get snacks and refreshment in the bar on the shady main plaza.

Just east of the village the AL140 branches right, leading to an area honeycombed with caves. Before reaching the hamlet of Los

Molinos del Río Aguas, a sign on the right indicates the parking lot for the Cuevas de Sorbas. Here you can make guided excursions of 90 minutes to four or five hours to galleries of gypsum dramatically eroded by underground streams. The crystals sparkle under your helmet light as you explore the caves.

Continue along the AL140, passing Los Molinos, and turn right on the N344 autovía. After 23 kilometres, swing right to visit Níjar. Orange and lemon trees and palms flourish in this oasis in the desert. The town is renowned for its rustic, hand-painted pottery and you will find a number of workshops and displays. Locally made handwoven blankets known as jarapas are also good buys.

An incident near Níjar in 1928 inspired Federico García Lorca to write one of his most famous plays, "Blood Wedding". Just before a girl named Paquita La Coja (Paquita the Lame One) was to get married, she eloped with her cousin. Relatives chased them and in a bloody act of vengeance the cousin was shot dead. Paquita's prospective groom felt so humiliated that not only did the marriage fall through but ever after he refused even to look at her photograph. She never married.

From Níjar, it is an easy 35-kilometre run on the N334 across the plain, dotted with greenhouses, to Almería.

WHAT TO SEE

Santa Fe de Mondújar:
Necrópolis de Los Millares, open Tues-Sat 9.30am-4pm, July 1-Sept 15 Tues-Sat 9am-3pm. Closed Mon. Tel: 608 95 70 65.

Tabernas:
Mini Hollywood, Ctra N340, km 364. Open daily March-September 10am-9pm, Oct-March 10am-7pm, closed Mon. Entry 15.60 euros, children 8.11 euros. Tel: 950 36 52 36.

Texas Hollywood, Ctra N340, Tabernas: Tel: 950 16 54 58. Open 9am-9pm. Entry 8 euros, children 5 euros.

Western Leone, Ctra A-92, C3326, km 378.9, Tabernas. Tel: 950 16 54 05. Open 10am-9.30pm. Shows daily, winter months only weekends. Entry 6 euros, children 3 euros.

Plataforma Solar (solar energy research station), Tabernas. Visits by prior arrangement. Call 950 38 79 00.

Sorbas:
Cuevas de Sorbas: Open 10am-8pm high season, 10am-6pm low season. Guides speak Spanish, English, French. Wear casual clothing and trainers. Entry 8 euros. Booking advisable, 950 364 704. Website: www.cuevasdesorbas.com

WHERE TO STAY

Níjar:
Montes, Avda Garcia Lorca, 26. Tel. 950 36 01 57. Basic, clean hostal. €

Pechina:
Balneario de Sierra Alhamilla. Tel. 950-31 74 13. 8,000. Rated a two-star hotel. Modern spa facilities at hot springs. Bubble baths, mudbaths, massages. €€

Turre:
Cortijo El Nacimiento. Tel. 950 52 80 90. Old farmhouse with simple but welcoming accommodation. Off road to Turre and Mojácar from N340. €

WHERE TO EAT
Roadside ventas, or take a picnic.

MORE INFORMATION

Almería:
Tourist office, Parque Nicolás Salmerón, esq. Martínez Campos. Tel: 950 27 43 55. Open Mon-Fri 9am-7pm, Sat-Sun 10am-2pm.

Sorbas:
Municipal tourist office, Calle Terraplén 9. Tel: 950 364 476.

On the Trail
of Columbus

Columbus monument at entrance to Huelva

FIVE CENTURIES AGO CHRISTOPHER COLUMBUS ARRIVED IN HUELVA PROVINCE, BEGGING FOR HIS SUPPER, HIS DREAMS OF DISCOVERY SPURNED. BUT HERE CAME THE TURNING POINT THAT WOULD PUT HIS NAME IN EVERY HISTORY BOOK. THIS TOUR INTRODUCES YOU TO THE LOCATIONS WHERE COLUMBUS PLANNED AND PREPARED HIS VOYAGE. EN ROUTE, WE VISIT ONE OF EUROPE'S MOST IMPORTANT WILDLIFE SANCTUARIES AND THE SHRINE OF EL ROCÍO, REVERED BY MILLIONS. WITH AN EARLY START IT CAN BE A BUSY ONE-DAY TRIP, BUT ALLOW AT LEAST TWO DAYS TO DO IT COMFORTABLY.

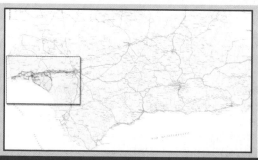

AREA: Coast of Huelva province
ROUTE: Seville→Bollullos del Condado→Coto Doñana→La Rábida→Palos→Moguer→El Rompido→Ayamonte→Niebla→Seville
DISTANCE: 370 kilometres

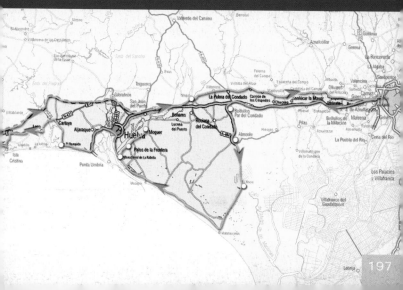

From Seville we head past the Isla de Cartuja, site of the 1992 world exhibition, and across the Guadalquivir River. The fast A49, the four-lane Autopista del Quinto Centenario, whisks us through undulating agricultural country with citrus and olive trees.

In Huelva province we enter the Condado wine country. Turn left on the A483 to Bollullos Par del Condado, 51 kilometres from Seville.

Bollullos (pop. 13,000) has long produced wines similar to sherry, but recently has developed lighter, fruity vintages. The first wine drunk in the New World by Columbus and his men almost certainly came from here. Several bodegas on the highway offer mosto - new wine direct from large barrels - and fresh seafood.

On Sundays during the season, January to July, El Gallo Bravo restaurant (Calle Picasso 17, tel. 959 40 82 35) is the scene of cockfighting championships. Stay clear if you can't stand blood sports - diners tuck into tasty seafood apparently oblivious to the mayhem in the cockpit.

Vineyards clothe much of the flat country between Bollullos and Almonte (pop. 15,000). In Almonte's agreeable main square, lined with palms and orange trees, storks nest on top of the church belfry.

South lies sandy terrain, covered with pines. We are entering Las Marismas, the wilderness of dunes and marshes at the mouth of the Guadalquivir. Fifteen kilometres from Almonte stands a bizarre township. With its single-storey dwellings, hitching posts and wide streets of sand, El Rocío resembles a Wild West ghost town.

Deserted most of the year, every Pentecost (usually in May) it is crammed with up to a million pilgrims. Most arrive by motor vehicle, but many trek on foot and horseback across marshes and dunes to pay tribute to the Virgin of Rocío, also known as the Blanca Paloma (the white dove) and the Queen of the Marshes. She stirs intense emotions and tumultuous scenes occur when the Virgin is finally carried out of her lofty white temple in the early hours of a Monday morning, to be paraded around for 12 hours or so.

According to legend, the image was found by a shepherd in the hollow of a tree six centuries ago. It mysteriously returned to the tree when he tried to carry it to Almonte, so a shrine was built here. Unless you are a member of one of the Hermandades (religious brotherhoods) that have their own accommodation, you will have to sleep in your car at romeria time.

Beyond El Rocío, on the right, you come to El Acebuche, the main centre for visitors to the Doñana National Park (see box for details).

Continue to the coast. At Matalascañas – this chaotic eruption of villas, hotels and high-rise apartments right next to an important wildlife sanctuary is an ecological aberration that makes no sense at all – turn sharp right on the A494, which runs 48 kilometres towards Huelva. A vast stretch of sandy beach lapped by the Atlantic lies beyond the umbrella pines to your left.

Beyond Mazagón, a summer resort with a fine beach and a number of bar-restaurants serving fresh fish, the N442 leads directly to Huelva. You know you are close when you see petro-chemical plants blighting the skyline.

Just before the road crosses the Río Tinto, turn right towards La Rábida, then left to the waterfront. Now you are really in Columbus territory. Tourist information is available at the entrance to botanical gardens on the road down to the Muelle de las Carabelas. Here you can visit an exhibition on "Colón" and his discoveries, including replicas of La Niña, La Pinta and the Santa María.

Near the quayside a statue of a winged man, erected by Argentina, pays tribute to four fliers, including General Franco's brother Ramón, who made a pioneer flight to Buenos Aires in 1926.

Probably the most significant Columbus site is the adjacent 14th-century Mudejar-style monastery, La Rábida, amid gardens overlooking the river. According to legend, he came here seeking food for his son Diego, telling the friars: "I am called Cristóbal Colón. I am a sea captain from Genoa, and I must beg my bread because kings will not accept the empires that I offer them."

The friars gave him a bed and he won over the prior and a friar-astronomer, who helped convince Spain's monarchs that a new route to the Indies was viable. A Franciscan monk shows visitors around the monastery, including the chapel where Columbus prayed to the Virgin of the Miracles before sailing into the unknown.

On the sandy soils around La Rábida, strawberry fields stretch for ever. This fruit ripens as early as February and thousands of tons are transported to European markets. During the strawberry season migrant workers of many nationalities are to be seen in the streets of Palos de la Frontera and Moguer.

A palm-lined avenue leads into Palos (pop. 7000). On Calle Colón (Columbus Street) stands the house of the Pinzón brothers who provided and crewed Columbus's ships. The facade is adorned with a coat of arms, two columns, and a plaque claiming that the discovery of the Americas was organised here.

Further along the street stands San Jorge Church, where Columbus and his crew attended mass before starting their epic voyage. They drew water for their ships from La Fontanilla, a brick-roofed well in gardens below the church.

But you will look in vain for the quayside from where the three caravels actually set sail. The river long ago became too silted for use at this point.

In the next town, laidback Moguer (pop. 15,000), where La Niña was built, you can wander through whitewashed streets to the 14th-century Gothic-Mudéjar convent of Santa Clara. On their return, Columbus and his men gave thanks here for safely riding out a terrible storm.

Wall plaques all over Moguer quote lines from the town's Nobel prize-winning poet Juan Ramón Jiménez (1881-1958). The fine old house where he spent his early years, converted into a museum, accommodates a library and many of his possessions, including 4000 books.

Semana Santa in Huelva

Opposite the Nuestra Señora de Granada church, a plaque quotes Jiménez's popular children's book "Platero and I" (translated into 50 languages): "The tower of Moguer, from nearby it looks like the Giralda seen from a distance." And indeed the church tower, around which wheel a pair of storks, does resemble Seville's Giralda in miniature.

As you drive into the rather undistinguished city of Huelva, on your left you see a massive monument dedicated to Christopher Columbus on a peninsula created by the Odiel and Tinto rivers. The sculpture by Gertrude Vanderbilt Whitney was a gift from the United States in 1929.

In the city, Columbus visited the Santuario de Nuestra Señora de la Cinta, a church founded in the 15th century. Also of interest are the quaintly English-style houses in the Barrio Reina Victoria built by the Río Tinto mining company early last century. Huelva's football club, El Recreativo, was the first in Spain, founded in 1879 after the British engineers introduced soccer in the peninsula.

Head for Punta Umbría and Ayamonte. The A497 soars over the Río Odiel, with docks on your left, and runs by the Marismas del Odiel. Some 200 species of birds are found in these marshes, including a large colony of spoonbills, flamingoes and herons.

On the Trail of Columbus

At the sea, a left turn takes you to Punta Umbría, a beach resort popular with Spaniards. Good seafood restaurants, but the unimaginative high-rise apartment blocks hardly make it worth a detour. Turning right, you drive past dunes, pines, sand - and big new tourist development. The Laguna de El Portil, just off the road, is a nature reserve with a rich variety of water fowl.

El Rompido, a fast-expanding fishing hamlet 25 kilometres from Huelva, is a relaxing spot to eat lunch while watching the boats rocking at anchor.

North of El Rompido, the road meets the N431 highway. Heading west, you bypass workaday Lepe (pop. 17,000). A sailor from Lepe, Rodrigo de Triana, was the first to sight land on the epic 1492 voyage to America.

Just as the English tell their Irish jokes, Spaniards joke about the leperos. In fact, it is the hardworking locals who are laughing as vast plantations of strawberries and citrus fruit have made them rich.

Fork left to visit Isla Cristina, so low lying on its sand spit that it seems about to disappear beneath the waves. Important for its fishing fleet, it also welcomes thousands of holidaymakers. Apart from its beaches, there is little to detain you.

Tourist development has also mushroomed at Isla Canela, a sand spit outside Ayamonte (pop. 17,000), the last town in Spain. Nostalgic types can still take the transbordador or ferry, which carries vehicles and passengers across the Guadiana river. Within 15 minutes you step ashore in Vila Real de Santo António in Portugal.

Now, however, a 700-metre bridge links the two countries and there are no border posts.

You can zip back to Seville on the A49 auto route or meander along via the N431 and A472. Definitely worth a stopover is Niebla (pop. 4000). This pleasant little town, east of Huelva, is surrounded by nearly two kilometres of glowering, 14-metres-thick

Niebla Castle

walls. In a park below the walls stands a giant metal statue of a dove with an olive branch in its beak.

Niebla was briefly the capital of a Moorish kingdom. Christian forces besieged the town for nine months in 1257, employing gunpowder, its first use on the Iberian Peninsula.

Information in English and Spanish leads you through the castle. Avoid the dungeons if you are squeamish. Chilling details—complete with gruesome sound effects—are offered about such tortures as breaking on the wheel, the saw and the hanging cage.

Just outside Niebla, the highway passes over a Roman bridge. Below flow the blood red, oxide-stained waters of the Río Tinto.

Your last stop on the A472 is Sanlúcar la Mayor, 12 kilometres before Seville. It lies in the Aljarafe, an area of fertile high ground above the Guadalquivir. "Five rivers flow from the Aljarafe," it was said, "of water, milk, wine, olive oil and honey".

Moorish influence is evident. Santa María church has three naves with horseshoe arches on square pillars and a tower from the Almohad era, while San Pedro has a similar tower and windows with horseshoe arches.

DOÑANA NATIONAL PARK

The Parque Nacional Doñana is one of Europe's most important nature sanctuaries. Embracing 76,000 hectares of dunes, oak and pine forest, lagoons and marshes, it offers protection for such endangered species as the imperial eagle and the lynx and is a vital breeding ground for thousands of water fowl. Spoonbills and flamingoes abound.

In the 16th century, when the Duke of Medina Sidonia (licking his wounds after commanding the not-so-invincible Armada) built a small palace in the park, it acquired the name of his wife, Doña Ana. For centuries it was a hunting ground for nobility and royalty. According to legend, while dallying there with Goya, an 18th-century Duchess of Alba – apparently impervious to the sabre-toothed mosquitoes – posed for his famous picture La Maja Desnuda (The Naked Woman).

Irrigation schemes, pollution, tourism development and new roads have all threatened the park, but environmental campaigns have awakened the public to the value of this unique sanctuary.

To visit the park interior, you must go on a four-hour guided tour in four-wheel-drives, starting from El Acebuche reception centre. The tours go every morning and afternoon except Mondays (June-Sept except Sundays). Reservation is essential. Fee: 18.70 euros. Contact the Centro de Recepción El Acebuche. Tel. 959 43 04 32/959 43 04 51. Open 8am-7pm, May-mid-Sept 8am-9pm.

You may actually see more wild life if you take a walk along marked paths from the visitor centres. These include: Palacio del Acebrón and La Rocina (off the El Rocío-Mataslascañas highway), José Antonio Valverde at Cerrado Garrido and Fábrica de Hielo (in Sanlúcar de Barrameda, see Excursion 11).

A private firm arranges visits to the park's northern zone by horse, four-wheel-drive or on foot. Contact 959 40 65 40.

WHAT TO SEE

Bollullos Par del Condado:
Museo del Vino, Plaza Ildefonso Pinto. Tel. 959 41 05 13. Open Mon-Fri 5-8pm. Call to arrange visits at other times. Winery visit included.

El Rocío:
Nuestra Señora del Rocío. Sanctuary holding the revered Virgin. Open 8.30am to sunset.

La Rábida:
Monasterio de la Rábida. Franciscan monastery where Columbus planned his voyage. Open 10am-1pm, 4-6.15pm. Sun 10.45am-1pm. Closed Mon. Entry 2.50 euros.

Muelle de las Carabelas. Tel. 959 53 05 97. Audiovisual, caravel replicas. Open Sept-April Tues-Sun 10am-7pm, other months closed weekday lunchtimes. Closed Mon. Entry 3 euros.

Parque Botánico "José Celestino Mutis", open Tues-Sun 10am-7pm. Entry 1.50 euros.

Moguer:
Casa Museo Juan Ramón Jiménez. Open 10am-2pm, 5-8pm. Closed Sun pm, Mon. Entry 1.80 euros. Nobel-winner's home.

Santa Clara, 14th-century Gothic-Mudéjar monastery. Museum of religious art. Tours on hour 11am-1pm, 5-7pm. Closed Sun, Mon. Entry 1.80 euros.

Niebla:
Castillo de los Guzmanes, 15th-century castle. Open 10am-6pm, June-mid-Sept 10am-10pm. Entry 4 euros.

Roman bridge.

Santa María de la Granada, 14th-century church built over 10th-century mosque.

Huelva:
Marismas del Odiel Park Visitors' Centre, Ctra del Dique Juan Carlos 1, km3, Tel. 959 50 02 36. Open Wed-Sun (Fri-Sun June 16-Oct 14). Reservations for visits by four-wheel-drive, tel. 959 50 05 12.

Palos De La Frontera:
Casa-Museo Martín Alonso Pinzón. Home of the Pinzón navigators. Open Mon-Fri 10.30am-1pm. Hours very "flexible" so call 959 35 01 99 to arrange entrance.

San Jorge, church where Columbus and crew prayed.

La Fontanilla, where Columbus filled his water casks.

BODEGAS (call first recommended):

Almonte:

Nuestra Señora del Rocío, Santiago, 69. Tel. 959 40 61 03. Tues-Fri 11.30am-1.30pm.

Bollullos:

Andrade, Avda Coronación, 35. Tel. 959 41 01 06. Mon-Fri 8am-3pm.

Cooperativa Vinícola del Condado, San José, 2. Tel. 959 41 02 61. 7am-1.30pm. *Iglesia,* Teniente Merchante, 2. Tel. 959 41 04 39. Mon-Fri 9am-2.30pm, 3.30-6pm. Roldan, Avda 28 Febrero, 111. Tel 959 41 44 49. 10.30am-1pm.

Palma del Condado:

Rubio, Palos de la Frontera, 14. Tel. 959 40 07 43. Mon-Fri 7am-1.30pm, 4-6pm.

WHERE TO STAY

Ayamonte:

Parador, El Castillito. Tel: 959 32 07 00). Commanding beautiful hilltop views over town and estuary. €€€-€€€€

El Rocío:

Toruño, Plaza del Acebuchal, 22. Tel. 959 44 23 23. Heart of El Rocío, next to lagoon. View wildlife from windows. Comfortable. Reservation essential in spring. €€€

La Rábida:

Hostería, Paraje de La Rábida. Tel: 959 35 03 12. Small hotel handy for monastery. Restaurant. €€

Mazagón:

Parador, Ctra Huelva-Matalascañas, km30. Tel: 959 53 63 00. Tranquil, amid pinewoods above sandy beach. €€€€

Moguer:

Immaculate budget accommodation at *Hostals Platero,* Aceña, 4, tel. 959 37 21 59, and *Pedro Alonso Niño,* Pedro Alonso Niño, 13, tel. 959 37 23 92. €

WHERE TO EAT

Ayamonte:
La Casona, Lusitania, 2. Tel: 959 32 10 25. Closed Sun in winter. Brick arches, wooden beams. Try the acedías (small flounder).

Bollullos del Condado:
Bodegón Reyes, Avda de la Paz, 2. Tel. 959 41 22 11. One of several bodegas serving fresh seafood, wine from the barrel.

El Rompido:
Caribe 11, Naos, s/n. Tel. 959 39 90 27. Closed evenings, except Fri-Sat & July-Aug. Fresh seafood washed down with chilled Bollullos white wine. Speciality: calamares del campo (onion rings and peppers).

Huelva:
Bar Azabache, Gobernador Alonso, 3. Tel. 959 25 75 28. Closed Sat, Sun. Excellent tapas, pork and fish dishes.

Moguer:
La Parrala, Plaza Monjas, 22. Tel: 959 37 04 52. Family-run restaurant, reasonable prices. La Parrala was a legendary cafe singer from Moguer, noted for her turbulent, passionate life.

MORE INFORMATION

Huelva:
Tourism office, Avda Alemania,12. Tel. 959 25 74 03. Open Mon-Fri-9am-7pm, Sat 10am-2pm.

Isla Cristina:
Tourism office, Calle Madrid, s/n. Tel. 959 33 26 94.

La Rábida:
Parque Botánico Celestino Mutis (Botanic Gardens), Plaza de las Monjas. Tel. 959 53 05 35. Open Tues-Sun 10am-7pm.

Moguer:
Castillo, Calle Huelva s/n. Tel. 959 37 18 98. Open Mon-Fri 10am-1.30pm, 5-7pm (summer 6-8pm)

Niebla:
Castillo, Tel. 959 36 22 70. Open 10am-6pm.

Land of Hams
and Silver

Iberian pigs grazing in the Sierra de Aracena.

MINERAL RICHES THAT HAVE FED MAN'S NEED AND GREED SINCE ANCIENT TIMES LIE IN THICKLY FORESTED UPLANDS BEHIND THE HUELVA COAST. THERE THE VISITOR DISCOVERS CASTLES AND CORK OAKS, SUBTERRANEAN WONDERS AND SPAIN'S MOST SUCCULENT HAMS. ALLOW AT LEAST TWO DAYS TO DO THIS TRIP COMFORTABLY.

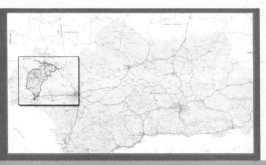

AREA: north of Huelva province
ROUTE: Huelva→Ríotinto→Aracena→Jabugo→Cortegana→Aroche→
Almonaster→Alosno→Huelva
DISTANCE: 300 kilometres

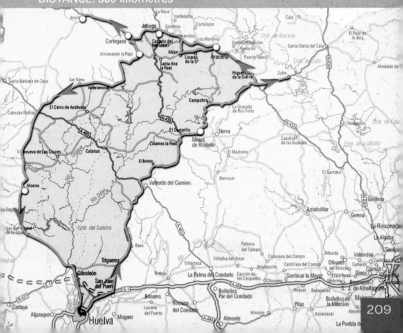

From Huelva, head north on route N435 towards Valverde del Camino and Aracena. At first you pass fertile farmland and vineyards, then increasing numbers of eucalypts and holm oaks as you enter the Andévalo, a transition area between coast and sierra with some of the world's richest mineral deposits.

Valverde, 45 kilometres from Huelva, spreads up a rise to your left. It is noted for its metal products and leatherwork, particularly sturdy boots. You climb into wilder forested country. Just after Zalamea la Real, fork right on A461 to Minas de Riotinto and Nerva.

Around these communities the earth has been gouged and riven since Phoenician and Roman times in the hunt for minerals. The fabled kingdom of Tartessos - said to have been "at the end of the world" though some archeologists place it near the Guadalquivir estuary - may have enriched itself from these mines.

British interests owned the mines until 1954 and at one time employed 10,000 workers. The British mine managers lived colonial-style, residing in Riotinto's Bella Vista suburb, with its leafy avenues, gabled villas and social club. For many years marriage with the "natives" was frowned upon, though workers did enjoy relatively advanced facilities,

Now apparently unviable, the mines have been converted into a tourist attraction. Visits can be made through the Museo Minero in Riotinto. The visit includes Bella Vista, a Roman acropolis, and the vast open-cast mines - one cut goes down 600 metres - from where copper, silver, gold and iron pyrites were extracted. The old mines railway runs but only on weekends and holidays.

To the north, an endless vista of rolling hills clothed in evergreens presents itself. Chestnut, apple and pear trees, elms and poplars flourish in well-watered valleys. This is the extreme west of the Sierra Morena and forms part of the Sierra de Aracena y Picos de Aroche Nature Park, which covers 184,000 hectares and reaches heights of around 1000 metres.

A slight detour eastwards from Riotinto on the A461 takes you to Zufre, spectacularly situated on a cliff edge. Its walls date back to the 12th century and traces of Arab influence abound.

Double back to the A433, turn west and soon you reach Aracena (pop. 6700), the capital of the sierra. The 13th-century church of the Knights Templar, a Mudéjar tower at one corner, is silhouetted against the skyline above this pleasant town. On Holy Thursday evening, a religious brotherhood bears the images out of the church and carries them down to the town in solemn procession.

Aracena's Gruta de las Maravillas (Cave of Marvels) attracts floods of visitors. A guided tour (minimum of 25 persons) conducts you along the galleries, past vividly coloured rock formations, 12 large chambers and six lakes. Look out for flesh-like curves in the Sala de los Desnudos and corny jokes from the guide.

Aracena's former town hall, a Renaissance-style building on Plaza Alta, has been restored to house an information office and exhibition on the nature park. Details are available of more than 600 kilometres of marked paths in the park, where you may sight vultures, imperial eagles, polecats, otters and much else.

Opposite the park office rises the massive Renaissance facade of Nuestra Señora de la Asunción. Only part of the church is in use. Work on restoring the whole edifice halted when a wealthy patron died.

Aracena is a handy base for visiting the sleepy villages of the sierra. The A470, which winds westwards through chestnuts and oaks, is one of Spain's most delightful rural drives. There are fine views from the sanctuary of the Virgin of Los Angeles above tiny Alájar. It is built on Arias Montano hill, named after a theologian and philosopher who lived many years here and was visited by King Philip 11 - look for the Sillita del Rey. A colourful romería to the shrine is held annually September 7-8.

A minor road winds northwards to picturesque Fuenteheridos, where water gushes abundantly from 12 spouts in a plaza fountain. Several bars and restaurants offer refreshment around the square.

In late autumn, business really mushrooms around here. Exotic fungi collected from the woods is shipped out for French gourmets, but plenty are also served in local bars as delicious, bargain-priced snacks. Interesting botanic gardens are located just outside the village at Villa Onuba, a residence run by Christian brothers and open to individual travellers looking for a peaceful spot (see Where to Stay).

Following the N433 west brings us to Galaroza, girdled with cherry and apple orchards. Wander along the main street and you encounter a monument to children splashing water, a reference to the annual Fiesta de los Jarritos on September 6 when villagers run riot dousing everybody in sight with water. In July a procession bears the Virgen del Carmen through the streets, unusual because Carmen is the patron saint of seafarers. And this image is obviously pregnant.

Throughout the sierra you will see thousands of dark brown Iberian pigs gorging on acorns among the cork oaks. The pigs' feet are black, thus the ham that comes from them is known as pata negra. This is Spain's most highly prized ham - and it sells at appropriately high prices. The genuine article has fat that is yellow rather than white and should melt in the mouth. The special flavour comes from the breed of pig, the *cerdo ibérico*, its diet and the long months of curing.

Dozens of villages produce excellent hams and sausages, each fiercely insistent that theirs is the best – Cumbres Mayores is an important centre. However, none can match the marketing success of Jabugo (just off the N433), once better known for its tobacco smugglers. Sánchez Romero Carvajal is the best-known producer and you will find a Jabugo street lined with bars and sales outlets.

Continue west to Cortegana (Corticata to the Romans). You can drive up to the restored 13th-century castle, with a 14th-century chapel next to it. Penetrate this town of 5000 people and you come to the fortress-like Divino Salvador parish church. Pigeons flutter about its lichen-crusted roof and small tiled spire. Three baroque ironwork pulpits adorn the interior.

A plaque on the church wall pays homage to Fray Alonso Giraldo de Terreros, "intrepid pioneer of the faith in North America". He founded the mission Río de San Sabas de los Apaches, but alas! he was killed by Comanche Indians in 1758.

In the nearby Plaza de la Constitución, the popular La Esquinita bar offers excellent tapas and wine at good prices.

Proximity to the Portuguese frontier made these sierra fastnesses strategically important. In 1236, Sancho 11 of Portugal laid siege to the fortress crowning Aroche (pop. 3500), 16 kilometres west of Cortegana, and ousted the Moors. The castle, with 10 towers, now accommodates a bullring.

Storks, sparrows and pigeons all find nesting space on the weathered walls of Aroche's Asunción church, which mixes Gothic and other styles. Those in reverent mood may want to seek out the unique Museo del Santo Rosario. Its owner has collected in his 16th-century house more than 1300 rosaries, presented by all manner of celebrities, including Mother Teresa, Archbishop Makarios, Richard Nixon and J.F. Kennedy. For visits to the local sights, contact official guide Manuel Amigo, at number 2, Calle Cilla (next to the town hall).

Returning to Cortegana, take the tortuous A470 through the hills to Almonaster la Real, some 600 metres above sea level. The tranquil village (pop. 2100) has the Gothic-Mudéjar church of San Martín and houses dating from medieval times. But the most outstanding sight is the beautifully proportioned 1000-year-old mosque, above the village within the battlements of a Moorish castle. Water bubbles in the entrance patio and the interior has five naves with brick arches, plus a mihrab (prayer niche). Traces of Roman and Visigothic materials can be found in this national monument.

Islamic communities hold prayers and meetings here occasionally, installing a market in the nearby bullring, an incongruous addition dating from 1891.

From Almonaster the fast way back to Huelva is via the N435. Alternatively, a little-frequented minor road from the village takes you via the hamlet of Gil Márquez through uninhabited pine-clad hills to the H120.

Interior of Almonaster's 1,000 year-old mosque

Head west towards Cabezas Rubias. The scrubby undulating country is dotted with eucalypts and scarred by mining near San Telmo. "Where nobody is a stranger" proudly proclaims the community of Cabezas.

Southwards, along the A495, the meadows between the oak trees are carpeted in wild flowers in spring, contrasting with the red rock riven by iron mining since Biblical times around Tharsis, a name to conjure with. In 1961 a small stone carving, known as the Mask of Tharsis, was discovered here. It is believed to date from 700 BC and some claim it portrays a king of legendary Tartessos.

A little south of Tharsis lies Alosno. It is unlikely to detain you long - unless you arrive during fiesta time as this village is famed for its many celebrations and its fandanguillos, a flamenco style said to be related to the jota of northern Spain.

Towards the coast, oaks and eucalypts give way to large plantations of strawberries and oranges.

WHAT TO SEE

Aracena:
Gruta de las Maravillas, open 10.30am-1.30pm, 3-6pm, 60-minute tours every hour, every half hour at weekends, entry 6.50 euros.
Museo de Arte Contemporáneo, open-air art show of modern sculptures.
Geological Museum, near the Gruta, open 10 am-1.30pm, 3-6pm.
Castle ruins and *Templars' church,* open 10am-8pm.

Almonaster La Real:
Moorish battlements and mosque, open daily 9am-7pm.

Aroche:
Fortress founded by Almoravids.
Museo Del Santo Rosario, Calle Alférez Carlos Lobo.
La Asunción, 13th-century church.

Cortegana:
Castle, open 11am-2pm, 5-7.30pm, closed Mon, entry 1.25 euros. 13th-century fortress.
Divino Salvador, 16th-century Mudéjar church.

Fuenteheridos:
Villa Onuba botanic gardens, open 10.30am-1.30pm, 4-6.30pm (later in summer). 120 species, some exotic.

Nerva:
Centro De Arte Moderno Daniel Vázquez Díaz, open 11am-2pm, 5-8pm, Sun & Mon open morning only.

Riotinto:
Museo Minero, Plaza del Museo. Tel. 959 59 00 25. Open daily 10.30am-3pm, 4-7pm. Entry museum 2.40 euros. Visits to mine installations, English quarter. Two-hour rail trip, Sat, Sun, holidays only, 8.41 euros.

Valverde del Camino:
Museo Etnográfico. Tel. 959 50 83 06. Open 11am-2pm, 5-8pm. Closed Mon. Exhibition in old English-style house. British, local life early last century, railways, shoe-making, metalwork.

WHERE TO STAY

Almonaster La Real:
Casa García, Avda San Martín, 2. Tel. 959 14 31 09. Tasteful modern facilities in small hotel at the village entrance. €€

Aracena:
Sierra de Aracena, Gran Vía, 21. Tel. 959 12 61 75. Comfortable, centrally located. €€

Finca Buen Vino, Ctra N433, km95, Los Marines. Tel. 959-12 40 34. Stylish mansion in 75 hectares of forest. Intimate country house atmosphere. English-run. Gourmet meals. Closed early July-early Sept. €€€€

Fuenteheridos:
Villa Turística, Ctra N433, km97. Tel. 959 12 52 02. Well-equipped individual units. Pool, restaurant. €€€€

Villa Onuba, Ctra N433, km97. Tel 959 12 51 35. Budget accommodation run by Marist Brothers. Mainly aimed at weekend groups, but individuals welcome weekdays. Small, comfortable rooms. Full, half pension available. Call first. €

WHERE TO EAT

Almonaster La Real:
Casa García. Excellent local dishes. Reasonable wine list.

Aracena:
Casas, Pozo de la Nieve, 41. Tel: 959 12 80 44. Famed for its regional ham and pork dishes.

La Capellanía, Ctra N433, km97. Tel. 959 12 50 34. Closed Mon & Sun-Thurs evenings Oct-May. A former convent. Pork products, with imaginative touches.

Jabugo:
Mesón Cinco Jotas, Ctra San Juan del Puerto. Tel. 959 12 10 71. Prime pork dishes reign supreme (cinco jotas is the term used for top-rated ham).

MORE INFORMATION

Almonaster:
Ayuntamiento, 959 14 30 03.

Aracena:
Tourist office, Plaza de San Pedro. Tel. 959 12 82 06. Open April-Sept 10am-2pm, 6-8pm, hours vary in winter.

Aroche:
Ayuntamiento, Tel.: 959 14 02 01.

Visitors' Centre, Sierra de Aracena y Picos de Aroche Nature Park: El Cabildo Viejo, Plaza Alta, s/n, Aracena. Tel. 959 12 88 25. Exhibition, information. Open daily 10 am-2pm, 4-6pm (later in summer).

Fuenteheridos

Into the Frying Pan

Storks nesting atop an Ecija church tower

SPRING AND AUTUMN—BUT DEFINITELY NOT SUMMER —
ARE GOOD TIMES TO VENTURE INTO THE FRYING PAN OF
ANDALUSIA, A REGION OF VAST ESTATES AND HISTORIC
TOWNS. ALLOW AT LEAST TWO DAYS FOR THIS TRIP.

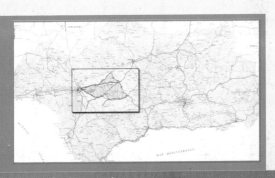

AREA: Seville province
ROUTE: Seville→Carmona→Palma del Río→Ecija→Estepa →Osuna
→Marchena→Sevilla
DISTANCE: 290km

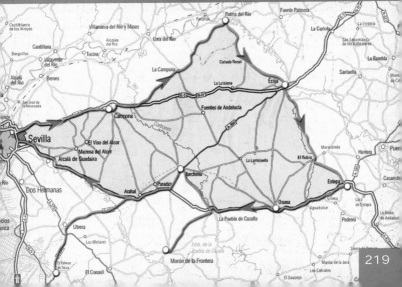

Take the N1V (E5) highway out of Seville towards Córdoba. Once free of the urban sprawl, this rolls across La Campiña, a vast plain watered by the Guadalquivir and its tributaries and a battleground for a succession of conquerors.

The fields seem to stretch into infinity, forming a vivid pattern of ochres and greens. Wheat, sunflowers, oranges, olives ripen under the strong sunshine.

Carmona (pop. 25,000) stands above the plain, 33 kilometres from Seville. Well-preserved noble residences, churches and convents combine to make the town a national monument. It was a fortress in Carthaginian times when it was named Kar-Hammon (city of the god Hammon, a sun deity).

Under Roman rule it sided with Caesar in his war with Pompey. Later it dominated a small Moorish kingdom. Its walls, reinforced by the Moors, are pierced by four Roman gates, the last discovered only in 1986.

Noble buildings abound in Carmona

In the newer part of town, you find the remarkable Necrópolis romana, excavated by British archeologist George Bonsor between 1881 and 1915. It has 900 family tombs dating back to 200 BC, including the Servilia, the size of a patrician villa, and the elaborate Elephant Tomb, with an elephant statue at its entrance.

From Carmona the A457 heads northwards, crossing the Guadalquivir to reach Lora del Río. Follow the A431 eastwards along the Guadalquivir - known to the Moors as Wadi al-Kabir, the Great River, but slow and muddy here. (Alternatively, from Carmona take the SE134, then CO132, to Palma del Río.)

Near the river, tobacco, cotton, and asparagus flourish. In cotton-picking time, October-November, travellers may blink on seeing snow along the roadside – actually cotton balls.

Twenty-four kilometres from Lora we reach Córdoba province. Turn right across the river, skirting orange orchards, to enter Palma del Río (pop. 19,000). Vestiges of 12th-century Moorish walls remain, but Palma is more celebrated as the birthplace of one of Spain's most controversial bullfighters, El Cordobés.

As a poor, barefoot youngster, he crept into the fields to practise fighting the bulls by moonlight. After his rise to fame, he returned to treat the whole town to drinks. Fighting bulls are still raised in the area.

The Hospedería San Francisco, a 16th-century monastery stylishly converted into a hotel and restaurant, is something of an oasis around here. The rooms are named after Californian missions - Fray Junípero Serra probably called here before going off to spread the faith in the New World.

The A453 leads southeast to Ecija. In spring, poppies splash crimson over the verges and the fields are a sea of green. But in summer farm workers begin their day at 6am and head for home by noon when temperatures climb to 45 degrees C and higher.

This is where the siesta really makes sense. You are in the Frying Pan of Andalusia. By September, when the fields are burned to dust, the locals are praying for rain.

Not for nothing does the next stop, Écija, boast on its coat of arms "City of the Sun - there is only one". Under clear skies, the 11 towers and 15 belfries of Écija - pronounce it "Etheeha" emphasizing the first letter - shimmer as in a mirage.

The "City of Towers"(pop. 35,000), on the banks of the Genil river, owes its origins to the Iberians. Astigi to the Greeks, it saw Roman, Visigoth and Moorish conquerors, but most of the town's monuments date from the prosperous 18th century.

Don't try driving around Écija. It's best to park and walk. Usually the Plaza de España, popularly known as El Salón (the lounge), is a favourite spot for strollers and flirters. However, the square may be partly closed due to a lengthy archeological dig that has revealed a large Moorish cemetery and Roman mosaics and baths.

Ecija lay on a main Roman highway, the Via Augusta. Ask to see the council chamber in the town hall. It's quite a sight - a dazzling seven-metre Roman mosaic from the 2nd century AD occupies pride of place below a 15th-century coffered ceiling.

Storks wheel about the tiled belfries of the many churches. A church or convent, each with art treasures, appears at every corner - Santiago, Santa María, Santa Cruz, del Carmen, and so on.

Herds of horses belonging to the military graze in the area around Écija. Take the A388 southwards to the village of Marinaleda. You are in the heart of La Campiña. The heat can be broiling, the estates are large and feudal aspects linger.

Entering Marinaleda a sign declares "Struggling for peace". The streets bear names like Che Guevara, Libertad and Salvador Allende. In the 1980s this village became a rallying point for the landless as the crusading mayor (still in office) led labourers in occupations of large estates.

Southeast, via SE735, you approach Estepa. Ostippo to the Romans, Istabba to the Moors, Estepa (pop. 12,000) today is Spain's cookie capital. Approaching Christmas, the air is sweet and heavy as many factories move into high gear to produce tons of *roscos*, *mantecados* and *polvorones*, sweet, crumbly biscuits.

Climb up through the old part of town, with its close-packed whitewashed houses, tiled roofs and ironwork balconies. A complex of convents and churches crown the heights above ancient walls.

The 16th-century Santa Clara convent has a beautiful patio. Knock on the convent door if you wish to buy delicious cakes made by the nuns. Modern marketing has arrived and you can now order their cakes through the convent's Internet site at www.santaclaraestepa.com

The fortress-like Santa María church next door, built on the site of a mosque, has a 15th-century Gothic interior.

Just below is the Balcony of Andalusia, a great viewing point for the patchwork panorama of La Campiña and the roofs and steeples of Estepa, including close at hand the elegant, free standing 50-metres-high Torre de la Victoria, a national monument.

An old refrain warns: *Si llevas dinero a Estepa, que ni el alcalde lo sepa* (If you take money to Estepa, keep it quiet – even from the mayor). But you will find today's townspeople friendly and helpful. In ancient times they gained fame for their heroism when the town was captured by the Romans in 27 BC. They set fire to the town and died in the flames rather than go into slavery.

West along the A92 through big sky country, we pass in early summer a countryside ablaze with wild flowers; rapeseed and sunflowers spread yellow carpets over the land.

After 24 kilometres you enter Osuna (pop. 18,000), one of Andalusia's best-preserved towns, bulging with splendid mansions – Calle San Pedro has some of the finest – and other monuments to past glory. Bears or *osos*) once roamed the area, from which the town's name is derived.

Philip 11 created the title Duke of Osuna in 1562 and the Osunas became one of Spain's most powerful families in the 17th and 18th centuries, accumulating more than 50 titles and vast land holdings. Their patronage enriched Osuna with architectural treasures.

*La Encarnación
Monastery, Osuna*

Cotton pickers in Córdoba

At the top of the town is the former university, founded in 1549 by the first duke's father. It is now a secondary school. Close by is the Colegiata de Santa María de la Asunción, an immaculately-restored Renaissance church with a beautiful columned patio, magnificent Mudéjar ceilings, ornate altars and five paintings by Ribera.

Look for the life-sized polychrome of the Virgin and Child. Her stomach hinges open to reveal a storage place for the host. Beneath the church is a pantheon, still in use by the Osuna family. The niches are small because they shelter only the bones.

At the last count, 18 nuns, many of them Colombians, lived in seclusion at the 16th-century Monastery de la Encarnación, just below the Colegiata. Its museum has many religious treasures, included polychrome carvings and rich brocades made by the nuns.

Stews and *ardoria*, a type of *salmorejo* (made of bread, olive oil, vinegar, tomato and salt and served cold), are typical local dishes.

The A92 auto route speeds you back to Seville. At La Puebla de Cazalla, make a detour along the A380 to ancient Marchena. The Seville Gate and Moorish walls date back to the 12th century, but Marchena's golden age came later under the Dukes of Arcos.

Park your car, wander the labyrinth of narrow streets and you will understand why Marchena bills itself as "The Unknown Beauty". You come across the Plaza Ducal, noble residences and many fine old churches and convents. If you fancy a night in a convent, check out Marchena's Hospedería Santa María.

You can also turn left at La Puebla to drive 20 kilometres on SE451 to Morón de la Frontera. The ruins of a Moorish fortress stand above the Gothic-Renaissance San Miguel church and steep streets. Nearby is a United States Air Force base.

Rejoin the A92 at El Arahal. Near Seville, the highway skirts Alcalá de Guadaira. Known to the Moors as Al Kalat Wad Aira, its impressive Almohad castle has seven of its 11 towers surviving.

Pope Gregorio's Cathedral, a detour to Utrera and El Palmar

A detour (southwest on the A364 leaving the A92 at El Arahal) takes you to the fiefdom of Andalusia's Pope.

You cross a featureless landscape to reach workaday Utrera (pop. 44,000), noted for olives and flamenco (the Potaje Flamenco held in June is a major festival). Worth viewing are the restored Moorish castle, the Gothic Santiago church, the 14th-century entrance gate Arco de la Villa and the 15th-century Santa María de la Mesa church with a splendid facade.

Take the A364 towards Jerez de la Frontera. After 15 kilometres, just outside El Palmar de Troya, you reach a massive concrete domed basilica behind high walls. Appearances of the Virgin here in 1968 and other miracles led to the creation of a bizarre sect headed by "Pope Gregorio XV11". This blind "hammer of heretics", who named Franco a saint, has followers in North and South America.

Minibuses arrive from Seville, bearing cardinals, bishops and heavily veiled nuns, for a daily 6pm mass, an astonishing affair in which dozens of priests perform elaborate rituals before more than 30 altars. To get past the dour guardians at the entrance you must have arms and legs well covered. Women must wear skirts, head scarves and "respectable" underwear.

WHAT TO SEE

Carmona:

Roman Necropolis and Museum, open 9am-5pm, Sat-Sun 10-2pm, closed Mon (closed Sun, Mon in summer).

Alcázar Puerta de Sevilla, open Mon-Sat 10am-6pm, Sun 10am-3pm, entry 2 euros, fortifications dating from Carthaginian and Roman times.

Santa María, open Mon-Fri 10am-2pm, 5-7pm, Sat 10am-2pm, closed Sun & Aug, Gothic church with patio from a mosque, historic exhibition; *Ayuntamiento*, open 8am-3pm, Roman mosaic in patio.

Ecija:

Palacio de Peñaflor. Curved facade with frescos. Patio, ground floor open Mon-Fri 10am-1pm, 4.30-7.30pm, Sat, Sun 11am-1pm.

Archeological museum, Palacio de Benamejí. Splendid 18th-century palace. Open Tues-Fri 9.30am-1.30pm, 4.30-6.30pm, Sat, Sun 9am-2pm. Closed Mon.

Cámara Oscura, Ayuntamiento, open Tues-Sun 10am-2.30pm. Entry 1.80 euros. Exhibition, panoramic views.

Las Teresas Convent, open 10am-1pm, nuns sell cakes.

Santa María, Santiago, Santa Cruz churches, open morning and evening daily.

Estepa:

Santa María church, with adjoining keep (Torre del Homenaje), founded in 14th century by Order of St James.

Torre de la Victoria, open Mon-Fri 10am-2pm, Mon-Wed 4-6pm, ask for key at Museo Archeológico.

Carmen church, Baroque splendour, dazzling facade.

Museo del Mantecado, open Sept-Dec (inquire at tourism office), shows manufacture of sweets.

Marchena:

Lorenzo Coullaut Valera Museum, open Mon-Fri 10am-6pm, Sat, Sun 11am-3pm. Housed in 12th-century Moorish tower. Sculptures, paintings of noted Marchena-born artist.

Zurbarán Museum, open Tues-Fri 10am-1pm (prior arrangement with tourism office), Sat, Sun 10.30am-1pm. Nine Zurbarán canvases, art treasures in 15th-century San Juan Bautista church.

Osuna:

Santa María de la Asunción. Guided visits 10am-1.30pm, 3.30-6.30pm, closed Mon. Entry 1.80 euros. 16th-century Renaissance architecture, Sepulcro Ducal. *La Encarnación,* a 16th-century monastery with beautiful patio. Guided visits, same hours as Santa María.

Old University, 16th century.

Museo Arqueológico, Plaza de la Duquesa.
Open 11.30am-1.30pm, 4.30-6.30pm.

WHERE TO STAY

Carmona:

Parador Nacional Alcázar del Rey Don Pedro. Tel: 954 14 10 10. Much-restored castle, once occupied by King Pedro the Cruel. Handsome patio, views, pool. €€€€

Écija:

Platería, Calle Platería, 4. Tel. 955 90 27 54. Immaculate small hotel, pleasant patio, restaurant. Off Plaza Salón. Parking tricky. €€

Estepa:

Manantial de Roya, Paseo de Roya. Tel. 653-92 44 56. Tranquil location by a spring 2km from town. Small hotel in traditional style. €€

Marchena:

Hospedería Santa María, Convento Purísima Concepción, Palacio Ducal, 9. Tel. 954 84 39 83. Comfortable accommodation in newly converted section of convent founded in 1624. €

Osuna:

Palacio Marqués de la Gomera, San Pedro, 20. Tel. 954 81 22 23. Splendid 18th-century palace converted to luxury hotel. Delightful patio. Bedrooms in different styles, those on top floor rather claustrophobic. €€€.

Caballo Blanco, Granada, 1. Tel: 954 81 01 84. Renovated old-style hostal. €€

Palma del Río:

Hospedería San Francisco, Avenida Pio X11, 35. Tel: 957 71 01 83. Converted monastery, featuring Roman columns and hand-painted tiles. €€€

WHERE TO EAT

Carmona:

San Fernando, Sacramento, 3. Tel. 954 14 35 56. Closed Sun night, Mon & Aug. Imaginative dishes served in an old mansion.

Ecija:

Bodegón del Gallego, Arcipreste Aparicio, 3. Tel: 954 83 26 18.

Closed Sun in summer. Agreeable Galician-style restaurant. Fresh seafood. Wood oven for roasts.

Osuna:
Palacio Marqués de la Gomera. Stylish dining in two restaurants. Mediterranean cuisine.

Mesón del Duque, Plaza de la Duquesa, 2. Tel: 954 81 28 45. Closed Tues, 2nd week May. Typical local dishes, good prices.

Recommended tapa bars are *Molinillo,* Plaza España, 10, *Reserva Mediterránea,* Carrera, 6, and *Taberna Raspao,* Plaza de la Merced.

Palma del Río:
Hospedería San Francisco. Upmarket restaurant in refectory. Renowned for game dishes.

MORE INFORMATION

Carmona:
Tourism office, Alcázar, Puerta de Sevilla, s/n. Tel: 954-19 09 55. Open Mon-Sat 10am-6pm, Sun 10am-3pm.

Ecija:
Tourism office, Ayuntamiento, Plaza de España. Tel. 955-90 29 33. Open 9.30am-3pm, 4-7pm.

Estepa:
Tourism office, Casa de Cultura, Saladillo, 12. Tel. 954 91 27 71. Open Mon-Fri 10am-2pm, Mon-Wed 4-6pm.

Marchena:
Tourism office, Las Torres, 40. Tel. 955 84 61 67. Open Mon-Fri 10am-6pm.

Osuna:
Tourism office, Plaza Mayor. Tel. 954 81 57 32. Open Mon-Fri 9am-2pm, 5-7pm.

Osuna Asociación Turístico Cultural. Tel. 954 81 28 52. Information, guided tours.

Palma del Río:
Tourism office, Cardenal Portocarrero, s/n. Tel. 957 64 43 70.

Exploring the
Wild Frontier

Tumbling water in Córdoba's far north

SIERRA MORENA ROADS ARE ABLAZE WITH WILD FLOWERS IN SPRING. THEY ARE ALSO TRULY VOLUPTUOUS - CURVES, CURVES AND MORE CURVES. DON'T OVERDO THE WINE AT LUNCH OR YOU MAY MAKE AN UNSCHEDULED DETOUR INTO THE CORK OAKS.

RELATIVELY FEW TOURISTS VENTURE INTO THIS MOUNTAINOUS BARRIER ALONG ANDALUSIA'S NORTHERN EDGE, REASON ENOUGH FOR A JOURNEY OF EXPLORATION. IT IS A REGION OF REMOTE VILLAGES, HARDY PEOPLE AND ABUNDANT WILDLIFE. ALLOW THREE DAYS AT LEAST FOR THIS TRIP.

AREA: Sierra Morena, north of Seville and Córdoba provinces
ROUTE: Seville→Cazalla→Constantina→Fuente Obejuna→Belalcázar →Pedroche→Pozoblanco→Villaviciosa→Córdoba
DISTANCE: 450 kilometres

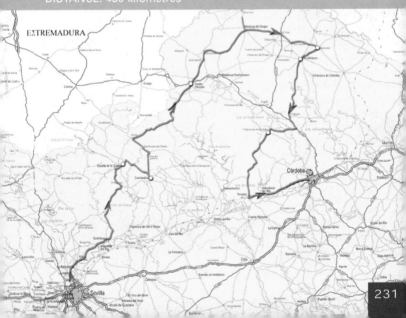

From Seville we head for the hills, taking the A431 to Alcalá del Río then turning north on the meandering C433 towards Cazalla de la Sierra. The country grows gradually wilder.

At El Pedroso, a halt on the Seville-Zafra rail line, you can eat heartily at the basic bar-restaurant Los Monteros. In season game will be on the menu and fried or roast *faisanes*, the tasty *boletus edulis* mushroom.

Thousands of deer and boar roam the undulating oak-dotted ranges in the north of Seville and Córdoba provinces, attracting hunters from all over Europe. In expensive "monterías" staged on vast estates, dog-packs drive the stags towards the hunters.

Seville's Sierra Norte, covering 164,000 hectares, has been declared a nature park. It's ideal for outdoor sports, such as hiking, fishing and biking. Consult the park information office on the Pedroso-Constantina road.

Continuing on the C433, between El Pedroso and Cazalla you encounter the imposing brick facade of an abandoned bodega,

Fishing at Pintado reservoir, near Cazalla

El Galeón. Weeds grow about its 114 huge vats where wine once matured.

When 70 local distilleries were making anise and cherry liqueur, the product was so famous that in parts of Latin America anise was referred to as El Cazalla. But the phylloxera bug destroyed the vines and olive trees replaced them. Now only two Cazalla producers of anise remain.

Pedro the Cruel is said to have hunted with the Black Prince around Cazalla de la Sierra (from the Arabic Kazala), a sleepy white town of 5000 inhabitants, 590 metres above sea level. It was the summer residence at one time of Spain's Felipe V, lured here no doubt by his passion for hunting. Now it is a favourite bolthole for *sevillanos*, looking for peace and fresh air.

Wandering its quiet streets, you come across distinguished old houses, San Agustín convent, closed and crumbling and for a time used as a distillery, and the fortress-like Consolación parish church. With a red-brick Mudéjar tower and Renaissance-style columns, it dates from the 14th century.

Conversing on a street in Constantina

Even more impressive is the Palacio de San Benito, an exclusive luxury hotel opened in 2002 that ranks among the most elegant in Andalusia. Although it appears as mellow as the 16th-century church alongside, the hotel is of new construction. Doors, columns, tiles, paintings were brought in from all over Spain and beyond to create a traditional atmosphere.

Three kilometres east of Cazalla, along a winding paved track off the A455 to Constantina, lie the remains of a 500-year-old Carthusian monastery. Follow the signs for La Cartuja and the Villa Turística.

Originally intended to accommodate retired monks from the wealthy monastery on Seville's Isla de la Cartuja, the monastery long sheltered travellers to and from Extremadura, but the vast Baroque structure with refectory and cloister fell into ruin when church property was confiscated in the 19th century.

An English adventurer bought the ruins in 1973, then passed them to a Spanish company, directed by Carmen Ladrón de Guevara. She has done a remarkable job of restoring much of the old structure and established an art gallery. At the monastery entrance, she runs the Hospedería de la Cartuja, a small hotel.

Continue along the A455 to Constantina, an agreeable town of 7000 inhabitants. Its name derives from the emperor Constantine the Great and in Roman times the famed local wine, known as cocolubis, was exported to Rome via the port of Seville. Silver and iron were once mined here. One of the town's most tragic moments came in 1810 when 300 residents were killed in a battle with Napoleon's troops.

Below the remains of a Moorish fortress tumble the whitewashed dwellings and narrow alleys of the Barrio de la Morería. A leisurely stroll along Mesones, the central, pedestrians-only street, takes you past fine old houses and Encarnación church, which boasts a handsome Renaissance door and a 50-metres-high tower.

King Juan Carlos is among celebrities who visit the area to hunt. However, despite what some guidebooks say, you are unlikely to encounter him dining with ordinary citizens at the Cambio del Tercio restaurant.

From Constantina you can return to the Guadalquivir valley and link up with Excursion 21 by heading south on the A455 to Lora del Río, 29 kilometres away.

But we are heading for remoter parts. The direct route north is via the SE163, although you can make a detour along SE150 to Las Navas de la Concepción, visiting pastures and woodland populated only by grazing pigs and sheep.

At Alanís, dominated by a hilltop fort, turn northeast on the A447 to Fuente Obejuna. This is one of Andalusia's wildest, loneliest roads. A sign warns "Carretera muy peligrosa". Don't attempt it at night. It is narrow, has no white lines or protective barriers, and has more wiggles than a model on the catwalk. Fortunately, traffic is very sparse.

After about 15 kilometres the oak forests give way to more open country, covered with shrubs. Red-legged partridge scuttle across the road. Hawks hover over hillsides glowing with spring colours, lavender, irises and millions of white rockroses. To the north you can glimpse Extremadura.

Suddenly, after entering Córdoba province, the road straightens into a real highway of dreamlike smoothness, built to transport nuclear waste to El Cabril storage plant (security is high, we're told). Fuente Obejuna appears, rising above wheatfields and green pastures.

Though not particularly distinguished, this town (pop. 6000) entered into legend after a rebellion against the ruling Order of Calatrava. In 1476, angry townsfolk killed the tyrannical Comendador Mayor Fernán Gómez de Guzmán, hacking his body to pieces in the main plaza. Interrogated later about who was guilty, the inhabitants allegedly replied as one: "Fuente Obejuna, señor!". And nobody was punished.

The playwright Lope de Vega immortalised the incident when he based his best-known work on it. Every two to three years (it was scheduled for August, 2003) the townspeople stage the play In the main square, named Plaza Lope de Vega, and Fuente Obejuna is swamped with visitors.

Fuente Obejuna breathes rural tranquillity - on a recent visit the big news on the town hall notice board was the start of a course on breeding snails. However, a plaque in the 15th-century Nuestra Señora del Castillo parish church, which towers over the square, recalls another violent event. At the start of the Civil War, 50 Catholics, including clerics, were killed here.

A local curiosity is the Casa Cardona, a Modernist palace with an ornate facade. Empty for many years, it is being restored for public use. In the surrounding countryside are 14 hamlets, each with its own customs and fiestas.

The landscape changes as we take the back roads, CP237 and CP222, to Hinojosa del Duque. It's flatter, with granite walls, storks and fewer trees. We're entering Los Pedroches, a zone reminiscent of Extremadura rather than Andalusia. The Arabs called it Fash al-Ballut (Land of the Acorns), and you'll see why.

Hinojosa is dominated by the "Catedral de la Sierra", the vast Gothic-Renaissance pile of San Juan Bautista church. Eight kilometres to the north an immense tower breaks the skyline. It belongs to the ruined castle of Belalcázar, built by the Sotomayors, masters of the Order of Calatrava, in 1466.

To survive in this somewhat bleak corner of Andalusia, the natives must have been as tough as the granite they used for so many buildings. One local boy escaped to the Americas. Sebastián de Belalcázar conquered Nicaragua and founded Quito, capital of Ecuador.

Santa Clara monastery, just outside town, appears little changed since those times. If you have a sweet tooth, pay a visit to buy the delicious cakes baked by the enclosed order of nuns. Colour pictures display what's available but the nuns stay out of sight. You pass your money through a revolving door.

Eastwards on the CP236, it's sheep and cornfields all the way to Santa Eufemia. Way above this village, eagles and vultures circle about Miramontes, a ruined 11th-century Arab fort. As of this writing, the 17 kilometres along CO 9026 towards El Guijo is one of the region's most potholed roads.

Head for Pedroche, a charming village above which rises the 56-metre tower of El Salvador, a Gothic-Mudéjar church built with stones from a demolished castle. Outside, a plaque commemorates the assassination of 95 persons, "fallen for God and for Spain" in July, 1936, but Pedroche, surrounded by dairy farms, is placid enough today.

When Pedroche was the local capital, mayors of seven municipalities used to meet at the Ermita de la Piedra Santa, just to the north. Battered wooden benches in the chapel bear the names of the villages.

To the south you enter industrious Pozoblanco, the largest town of Los Pedroches. Ginés de Sepúlveda, chronicler of Felipe 11, is buried in Santa Catalina church, but most Spaniards know of Pozoblanco only through a tragic bullfight on September 26, 1984.

Paquirri, one of the country's most popular matadors, was gored by Avispado (Wide Awake), a black bull, and died as he was being rushed to hospital in Córdoba.

Journeying south, we follow the N502 to the Guadiato valley. This is an area of great natural beauty, though mining activity, now abandoned, left its scars. Peñarroya Pueblonuevo, the largest centre, is attempting to turn its old industrial installations into a tourist attraction, with a mining museum. And Bélmez, overlooked by a 13th-century castle, offers everything from hiking to water sports.

You can speed into Córdoba on the N432, but a delightful alternative takes you along the A433 into the hills above the Guadiato river. At Villaviciosa de Córdoba, you can visit the bodega of Gómez Nevado, which has been producing sherry-type wine since 1754.

From here the A433 winds 44 kilometres down to the Guadalquivir and main Córdoba highway at Posadas, passing through the Sierra de Hornachuelos nature park. This beautiful route resembles a country lane, bordered by forests of oaks and pines and with virtually no traffic. You can catch glimpses of woodpeckers, magpies, bee-eaters, hoopoes, quail. A great area for picnics.

WHAT TO SEE

Belalcázar:
15th-century castle ruins; Santa Clara de la Columna monastery, founded 1476, cakes on sale 9.30am-1.30pm, 4.30-6.30pm.

Cazalla de la Sierra:
Consolación, 14th-century church; *Ermita del Monte*, Baroque splendour, open daily except Thurs.

La Cartuja, off A455, km3.5. Restored monastery and art gallery. Open 10am-2pm, 4-8pm. Entry 3 euros.

Constantina:
Santa María de la Encarnación, Renaissance *Puerta del Perdón*, tower designed by Hernán Ruiz; remains of *Almoravid fort*.

Fuente Obejuna:
Nuestra Señora del Castillo, beautiful Renaissance-style altarpiece; *Casa Cardona*, Modernist palace with an ornate facade.

Hinojosa del Duque:
San Juan Bautista, 15th-century Gothic, magnificent Plateresque entrance.

Pedroche:
El Salvador, 16th-century church.

Villaviciosa de Córdoba:
Wine-tasting at *Bodegas G. Gómez Nevado*, M. Arribas, 104. Tel. 957 36 00 96.

WHERE TO STAY

Belalcázar:
La Bolera, Padre Torrero, 17. Tel. 957 14 63 00. Simple, friendly

hostal in area where overnight options are few. En suite bathrooms.
Budget restaurant. Internet connection. €

Cazalla de la Sierra:

Palacio de San Benito, San Benito, s/n. Tel. 954 88 33 36. Palatial
luxury in traditional style. Nine rooms. Restaurant for guests only.
€€€€

Hospedería de la Cartuja, Ctra de Constantina. Tel. 954 88 45 16.
Intimate small hotel. Birdwatching, riding, art courses. €€€

Villa Turística, Ctra de Constantina, km 3.5, Cazalla de la Sierra.
Tel. 954 88 33 10. Stone cabins. Pool, restaurant. €€€

Constantina:

La Casa, José de la Bastida, 25. Tel. 955 88 01 58. Tiles, ironwork
adorn this renovated traditional Andalusian house with friendly
owners. Restaurant serves local dishes. €€

Casa Grande, Ctra Constantina-Cazalla, km1. Tel. 955 88 16 08.
Farmhouse built 1875, lovingly converted by retired Seville doctor
into stylish six-room hotel. Pool, gardens, outdoor activities.
Reasonably priced menu of the day. €€€€

Fuente Obejuna:

El Comendador, Luis Rodríguez, 25, tel. 957 58 52 22. Friendly,
comfortable hotel with restaurant. €

Pozoblanco:

Los Godos, Villanueva de Córdoba, 32. Tel. 957 77 02 00. One-
star hotel, centrally located with parking. €€€

Mirador, Ctra Pozoblanco-Añora, km1. Tel. 957 77 17 54. Simple
roadside hostal just outside town. Restaurant. €

WHERE TO EAT

Belalcázar:

Hostal La Bolera. Pork and game. Cheap menu.

Cazalla:

Posada del Moro, Paseo del Moro, s/n. Tel. 954 88 48 58. Game
dishes in stylish surroundings.

Constantina:

Mesón La Piedra, Ctra 432, km 70. Tel. 955 88 01 11. A phallic rock stands outside this converted bodega. Venison stew, mushrooms, cheap menu;

Cambio del Tercio, Virgen del Robledo, 51. Tel. 955 88 10 80. Specialities include stuffed partridge and pheasant.

Fuente Obejuna:

Hotel El Comendador. Pork and game.

Pozoblanco:

Pork and lamb dishes are popular in local restaurants, which include – *Don Marcos*, Marcos Redondo, 32. Tel. 957 77 09 50; *La Cepa*, Avda Villanueva de Córdoba, 20. Tel. 957 13 10 68; and *La Taberna*, Avda Villanueva de Córdoba, 28. Tel. 95 77 70 258.

MORE INFORMATION

Cazalla:

Tourism office, Tel. 954 88 35 62. Open Wed-Fri 10am-2pm, Sat-Sun 10.30am-2.30pm.

Constantina:

Tourism office, Ayuntamiento. Tel. 955 88 12 97.

Fuente Obejuna:

Tourism office, Town hall library. Tel. 957 58 45 60. Ask for Alfonso Fernández.

Guadiato valley:

Tourism office, Area de Turismo, Mancomunidad de Municipios, Peñarroya-Pueblonuevo. Tel. 957 56 70 22. Internet: www.valleguadiato.com

Sevilla:

Provincial tourism office (Turismo de la Provincia), Plaza del Triunfo, 1. Tel. 954 50 10 01.

Sierra Norte Nature Park: El Robledo Visitors' Centre, Ctra. Constantina-El Pedroso, km1. Near Constantina. Tel. 955 88 15 97. Open Thurs-Sun (Fri-Sun June 15-Oct 15). Exhibition, audiovisual.

Sheep in Sierra Morena

Virgen de la Cabeza Romería, north of Andújar

Pozoblanco: a name known to all bullfight fans

The Sunflower Route

Farmhouse and flowers in Córdoba's Campiña region

SOUTH OF CÓRDOBA LIES LA SUBBÉTICA, AN AREA OF RUGGED BEAUTY, BAROQUE SPLENDOUR AND HISTORIC OLD TOWNS. IT INCLUDES A 31,000-HECTARE NATURE PARK WITHIN WHOSE BOUNDARIES ARE MOUNTAINS RISING TO 1500 METRES.

AREA: southern Córdoba province
ROUTE: Córdoba→Baena→Priego de Córdoba→Cabra→Lucena →Montilla→Córdoba
DISTANCE: 220 kilometres

The N432, running south-east from Córdoba along the Guadajoz River, takes you first across the undulating, treeless Campiña region. In spring and early summer this is a blazing carpet of sunflowers and dark-green foliage, interspersed with the lighter green of ripening wheat. By late summer it has been charred brown.

Espejo (pop. 5000) is the first place of any size. Its medieval fortress, belonging to one of Spain's largest land-owning families, the Dukes of Osuna, dominates the town and surrounding vineyards.

In nondescript Castro del Río (pop. 7800) ask at the town hall to see the room where Cervantes, during his tax-collecting days, was tossed into jail for a week for overstepping the mark.

Fields of garlic, artichokes, wheat and barley flicker past. Approaching Baena, 62 kilometres from Córdoba, olives take over. The quality of Baena's olive oil was already a byword 500 years ago. Baena (pop. 19,000) is a dazzling snow cascading down a hillside. Within it, you will find notable examples of Gothic and Renaissance art. Nervous drivers should leave their cars in the lower quarter and ascend the steep, narrow streets on foot.

Holy Week processions are deafeningly impressive in Baena, as the whole town trembles to the thunder of 7000 drums.

Santa María la Mayor church crowns the top of the town and nearby is the ancient Madre de Dios convent. At a side door, around Christmas and Easter (8am-2.30p, 4-7.30pm), you can buy cakes made by the few remaining Dominican nuns. You receive the cakes via a turntable that ensures outsiders and cloistered nuns never see one another.

One side of the Plaza de la Constitución, reconstructed to create an underground parking lot, is bounded by the brick facade of the new town hall. On another side an old arcaded building, once a tax office, then a Civil Guard barracks, now shelters the Mesón Casa del Monte. In the brick-arched dining room, you can sample local dishes. Baena's wine is similar to sherry. Ask for the excellent fino Cancionero, aged eight years in the barrel.

About three kilometres along the N432 out of Baena, look for a new road to the right leading to Zuheros. Entering the Sierras Subbéticas, you pass a hamlet named Marbella. Cross the A316 and then follow a winding road up to Zuheros, dramatically situated on a spur on the edge of the nature park, an area of limestone crags, oak trees and wild life.

Weave your way through the whitewashed village to the parish church and jutting arrogantly above it the battlements of a 16th-century castle. Nearby is an archeological museum that holds ceramics, arrow heads, and other artefacts.

But Zuheros is best known for its Cueva de los Murciélagos (Cave of the Bats), reached by a four-kilometre road that curves above the village and offers views of the Bailon river gorge. Not explored until 1937, the cave was inhabited in Neolithic times and wall paintings remain. There's an information point 300 metres up the road to the cave.

From Zuheros, head east to Luque. A Moorish fort crowns one crag above the town, an antenna another. Continue on the CP72 past Fuente Alhama to join the A333, turning right to Priego de Córdoba. Old watch-towers crown one or two of the hills to the right. We squeeze through Las Angosturas, a narrow ravine, and head across an irrigated plain towards Priego de Córdoba.

Grape harvest

Priego is a snugly prosperous town with some magnificent buildings, many dating from the 18th century when its silk industry flourished.

From the Plaza del Ayuntamiento wander up Calle del Río, lined with noble mansions with imposing front doors and ironwork. The tourism office - headed by the helpful José Mateo, a true enthusiast for his town - is at Number 33, the house where Niceto Alcalá-Zamora, president of the Second Republic, was born.

The curving street ends at the Fuente del Rey, a king among fountains. Built between the 16th century and 1803, it has 139 spouts gushing into three pools, with Neptune in the centre.

To explore the rest of the town, head for the Barrio de la Villa. On the edge of this medieval quarter is the parish church of La Asunción, a national monument dating from 1525. The extravagant sacristy chapel is a mind-blowing piece of Baroque art.

Behind the church is a labyrinth of immaculately whitewashed, astonishingly narrow streets. Geraniums and petunias run amok on balconies and on patio walls. Eventually, like a cork popped from a bottle, you burst out on to the Adarve, an iron-railed promenade where lovers flirt and you can gaze over the surrounding countryside.

Wandering the streets of Priego, you encounter a series of magnificently adorned churches, such as the over-the-top Baroque of La Aurora. Every Saturday midnight the cloaked Hermanos (brothers) de la Aurora walk through the streets singing in praise of the Virgin and collecting alms.

From Priego you can make a side-trip on the A340 to Alcalá la Real (pop. 20,000) in Jaén province, crowned by La Mota, a fort built by the Moorish kings of Granada 700 years ago and rebuilt in the 16th century. Within the walls are two churches. Santo Domingo de Silos is 14th century Gothic-Mudéjar-Renaissance and Santa María la Mayor, heavily restored, was designed by Diego de Siloé.

Another brotherhood of the Aurora sings in the streets of Carcabuey, perched on a hump eight kilometres west of Priego.

From the Ayuntamiento the stepped Castillo and Virgen streets lead up to the castle. Near it is a vaulted Roman dungeon. Between dungeon and castle rises a monument to 20th-century sensitivity - a lofty electricity pylon.

Dozens of cats stand guard over the castle chapel sheltering Carcabuey's patron saint, the white-robed Virgen del Castillo. Discarded crutches by the altar and many ex votos testify to the Virgin's powers.

From Carcabuey take the A340 west. A side-road will take you to the Virgen de la Sierra shrine, a hilltop temple that attracts many pilgrims, including gypsies attending the Romería de los Gitanos in June.

To the right of the A340 lies Cabra, at the geographical centre of Andalusia. Near the castle is Asunción church, built in the 15th century over a mosque. It has magnificent Baroque choir stalls and an altar of red and black jasper. If you're looking for a picnic spot, head for La Fuente del Río, a pleasant tree-shaded area on the edge of town on the Priego road. Public swimming pools are nearby.

Further west, amid olive groves and fields of grain, we come to Lucena (pop. 32,000), noted for its furniture and brass and copperware. Several potters also work away, turning out botijos - earthenware drinking vessels - and other traditional pots.

Under the Caliph of Córdoba, Lucena, with its prosperous community of Jewish merchants, enjoyed virtual independence. The site of the mosque and an academy of Talmudic studies is said to be Santiago church, a national monument. In the last days of the kingdom of Granada, the Moorish king Boabdil was imprisoned in Lucena's Torre del Moral.

Five kilometres out of town the sanctuary of the Virgin of Araceli occupies a 868-metre-high hilltop, from where there are excellent views of the surrounding countryside. In April the Virgin is carried down to the church of San Mateo amid great emotion and excitement and on the first Sunday in May the Fiestas Aracelitanas are celebrated to pay due homage.

From Lucena, the N331 proceeds north over a sun-baked, undulating landscape. A lofty clock tower stands high above Aguilar de la Frontera (pop. 13,500). The Torre del Reloj, a fine brickwork structure, was built in 1774. Thread your way through Aguilar's narrow streets to the unusual eight-sided plaza of San José, on which are the Ayuntamiento and El Tuta tavern, meeting place of writers and wine imbibers.

Bird-watchers can trek four kilometres along the A309 to the Laguna de Zonar nature sanctuary.

This area is the heart of the officially denominated region of Montilla-Moriles wine, produced by the same methods as sherry (see Excursion 11 for details). Montilla's largest bodega, Alvear, welcomes visitors, as does Pérez Barquero, whose *amontillado* and *oloroso* are among the highest rated of Montilla wines.

Long narrow streets penetrate the heart of Montilla (pop. 23,000), birthplace of the great warrior El Gran Capitán, but with few outstanding sights. The public library is housed in the building where Garcilaso de la Vega, a Spanish Inca, laboured over his translations and works on the Inca empire. La Casa del Inca is on Capitán Alonso de Vargas, 3.

Horse Trek in Córdoba

Sunflowers, grains, and more sunflowers take over from vines north of Montilla. Ceramics freaks can turn left to the town of La Rambla where dozens of family firms turn out brightly decorated jugs and vases. Makers of the more restrained traditional styles are a dying breed.

Head back to the N331 to reach Montemayor, a sleepy town with a 16th-century parish church. Beneath the church is the Museo de Ulia, a museum of artefacts, mostly Roman. It's the personal collection of Don Pablo, the veteran parish priest, who lives alongside and has the key. Behind the church is an esplanade with a fine view of country and castle, the latter owned by the Duquesa de Frias. From Montemayor, it is a short run to Córdoba.

WHAT TO SEE
Baena:
Santa María la Mayor, Gothic church, founded 15th century.

Madre de Dios convent church, founded 1510, marble altar, paintings of Flemish and Italian origin.

Lucena:
Santiago, open Mon-Fri 8.30am-1pm, 6.30-9pm (weekends 7-8.30pm) hours vary in summer. National monument.

Montilla:
Bodegas: Alvear (Tel. 957 66 40 14). Visits 10.30am-1.30pm, 4.30-8.30pm. English, French German, Swedish spoken; *Pérez Barquero* (Avenida Andalucía, 27. Tel. 957 65 05 00). Call first.

Priego de Córdoba:
Iglesia de la Asunción, open 11am-1pm, 5.30-7.30pm, church founded 1525, Baroque refurbishment in 18th century, sacristy is a masterpiece.

Carnicerías Reales, to visit ask at tourism office, 16th-century market, slaughterhouse, fine patio.

Castillo, Arab fortress with later additions, exterior only.

Zuheros:
Cueva de los Murciélagos. Guided visits Sat, Sun, holidays. Oct-March 11am-5.30pm, April-Sept 11am-7.30pm. Groups can book weekday visits (call 957 69 45 45, 10am-2.30pm weekdays).

Museo Arqueológico, Calle Nueva, 1. Open weekends 10am-2pm, 4-6pm (hours vary weekdays and summer). Entry to cave, museum, castle 4.21 euros.

WHERE TO STAY

Baena:
Ipanuba, Nicolás Alcalá, 9. Tel 957 67 00 75. Modern, brick-fronted two-star hostal. €€

Lucena:
Santo Domingo, El Agua, 12. Tel: 957 51 11 00. An 18th-century convent converted into a four-star hotel. Magnificent patio. Superior cuisine in the hotel restaurant. €€€-€€€€.

Montilla:
Don Gonzalo, Ctra Madrid-Málaga km 447. Tel: 957 65 06 58. Three-star hotel, pool. €€

Priego de Córdoba:
Hostal Rafi, Isabel La Católica, 4. Tel. 957 54 07 49, Reasonably priced two-star hostal near town centre. €

Villa Turística, Aldea de Zagrilla, 7km from Priego.
Tel: 957 70 35 03. Village-style, delightful tranquil location, pool. Recommended restaurant. €€€

Zuheros:
Zuhayra, Mirador, 10. Tel. 957 69 46 93. Immaculate two-star hotel with restaurant. €€

WHERE TO EAT

Baena:
Mesón Casa del Monte, Plaza de la Constitución. Tel. 957 67 16 75. Closed Mon. Tapa bar-restaurant. Try revuelto de la casa (scrambled eggs with asparragus, broad beans, and onions).

Cabra:
Mesón del Vizconde, Martín Belda, 16, Cabra. Tel. 957 52 17 02. Closed July. Fast, friendly service. Specialities include aubergines stuffed with salmon.

Montilla:
Las Camachas, Ctra Córdoba-Málaga km 45. Tel. 957 65 00 04.
Popular restaurant. Try lamb baked with honey.

Priego:
La Fuente, Zagrilla Alta (near the Villa Turística). Tel: 957 703 734.
Sit outside under plane trees to the music of gushing water. Rabbit
or stewed kid. Priego tapa bars worth trying include *Bar Morales*
(Calle Dean Padilla, 7), with pavement tables, *Los Colorines* (Calle
Mesones, 8) and *Taberna Flamenca* (Calle Río, 50), where you may
catch flamenco singing.

MORE INFORMATION

Priego de Córdoba:
Tourism office, Río, 33,. Tel. 957 70 06 25. Open Tues-Sun
10am-1.30pm, 5-7.30pm, closed Sun pm and Mon.

Lucena:
Tourism office, Castillo del Moral, s/n. Tel. 957 513 282. Open
9am-2pm, 5-7pm (Mon), 5-9pm (Tues-Fri), weekends 11am-2pm,
6-8pm.

Cabra:
Interpretation Centre, Parque Natural de las Sierras Subbéticas,
A340, km 57, Cabra. Tel: 957 33 40 34.

Gypsy Fiesta near Cabra

Sierra Sanctuaries

Las Ermitas in the hills above Córdoba

WHEN THE SUMMER SUN HAMMERS CÓRDOBA AND THE TOURISTS DESPERATELY SEEK RELIEF IN CAFES AROUND THE MOSQUE, SENSIBLE CORDOBESES HEAD FOR THE HILLS. THE SIERRA MORENA RUNS RIGHT UP TO THE CITY'S EDGE AND ITS BREEZY HEIGHTS AND THICK WOODS ARE ONLY A FEW MINUTES AWAY.

THIS TRIP WILL BRING YOU TO PLEASANT PICNIC SPOTS, WAYSIDE RESTAURANTS, A POTENTATE'S DREAM PALACE, AND THE ANCIENT SANCTUARIES OF MEDIEVAL MYSTICS.

AREA: west and north of Córdoba
ROUTE: Córdoba→Madinat al-Zahra→Las Ermitas→Córdoba
DISTANCE: 80 kilometres

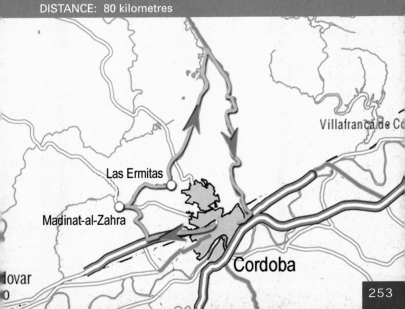

Take the A431 from Córdoba, which heads west along the Guadalquivir valley towards Almodóvar del Río and Seville. Follow the signs to Madinat al-Zahra. After five kilometres turn right. The road runs up a ridge for two kilometres to the ruins of a sumptuous residence created by the Caliph of Córdoba, Abd al-Rahman 111, in the 10th century, and named after his favourite wife.

Although exploration and restoration have been going on for years at Madinat al-Zahra, so far under a fifth of the ruins have been excavated. But enough of the jigsaw has been put together to give an idea of the splendour of the retreat where the Caliph retired with his concubines, slaves and dancing girls,

More than 10,000 men built the palace, employing 15,000 mules and 4000 camels to haul up the material to a point overlooking the fertile valley. The complex was on three levels, including gardens, a mosque and the Caliph's residence. Here he could listen to the tinkling fountains and take his ease amid halls of marble and jasper, decorated by leading craftsmen from Córdoba, at that time Europe's largest city.

Magnificent functions were held, at which awed visitors walked over precious carpets between lines of slaves and soldiers and admired a shimmering pool of quicksilver in the great reception chamber. Construction of the palace marked the zenith of the Omeya dynasty's rule in Andalusia, but it endured only a few years. In 1010 Berber invaders sacked it and over the centuries it was ransacked for building materials.

After strolling through the ruins and the restored sections, which can only hint at the richness of the Caliph's court, return to your car and continue uphill, towards Santa María de Trassierra and Las Ermitas (CP19). To the left, as you climb into the sierras past oak-dotted slopes, you will glimpse the San Jerónimo monastery in a commanding position.

At a crossroads, near a petrol station, the Restaurant El Cruce offers refreshment and shade under the trees. To the right a scenic road takes you directly back to Córdoba. Five kilometres to the left, past

Sierra pastures ablaze with flowers

private houses sheltering amid cork oaks, eucalypts and umbrella pines, lies the sleepy settlement of Santa María de la Trassierra.

However, we head directly across the junction towards Las Ermitas, passing over a pleasant wooded plateau. A kilometre or so from the crossroads, a short detour takes you to a *mirador* (lookout point). Continuing, you know you are approaching the hermitages as granite crosses by the roadside mark the way.

Las Ermitas are a closed world of meditation, harking back to early times. Christian hermits are said to have established themselves in caves in these mountains in 400AD. In the 16th century, the Council of Trent formed them into a single community near the San Jerónimo monastery.

Around 1700, the community moved to the present site, remaining there until 1957, when it finally died out. Since then the Carmelites have looked after the hermitages and only a few monks are in residence.

It is a tranquil spot, on a rocky promontory studded with pines, cypresses and cedars. High above Córdoba and the Guadalquivir, you can enjoy the clear air and magnificent views over the city.

Explanatory pamphlets are available in Spanish and, if not out of print, tortured English. An avenue of cypresses leads to a cross in memory of the Conde de Torres Cabrera, "remarkable protector of this venerable desert". Below the cross is a small iron grill. Peer through it and you are confronted by a grinning skull.

Read the inscription to get the message: "As you now see yourself, I saw myself./As you see me now, you will see yourself./Everything ends this way, Think about it and you will not sin."

As you ponder this sobering thought, carry on along a path to an example of the 13 hermits' cells. These are spartan affairs, with three sections, for reading, praying and resting. The wooden beds are covered only with thin esparto mats, in line with a sign that exhorts the faithful: "*Punish your body but castigate your will more.*" Each cell had a small garden for growing fruit and vegetables.

Beyond a small cemetery lies the church, dating from 1732. A wall plaque records that Queen Isabel 11 with her son Alfonso, the future king, visited on September 16, 1862.

Another skull greets you in the church entrance. This was used by Brother Juan de Dios, Marqués de Santaella y Villaverde, as a plate and drinking vessel. The English pamphlet explains why: "Doing so penitence for his before licentious life." He died at 49 in 1788 and you can see his likeness among the oil paintings of senior hermits inside.

The church is richly decorated with intricate carvings and an abundance of gold leaf, ivory and alabaster. Insert a coin near the entrance and lights flick on to reveal details of the altars, sculptures, oil paintings and a crucifix made of cinnamon.

Back in the shady gardens, you will find steps leading down to an esplanade from where you can feel the breeze and contemplate the Guadalquivir valley and the Campiña (the Córdoba plain), a patchwork of green, yellow and brown. Above the esplanade stands a huge statue of Christ.

Anybody wanting to spend some time in tranquil solitude and contemplation can stay at the hermitage. If you are interested, call 957 33 03 10.

Beyond Las Ermitas, the road continues past a forest of cork oaks to a junction with the Córdoba to Villaviciosa road, the CO110. Here stands the large Assuan restaurant and La Cabaña barbecue area. Las Dos Columnas, another popular restaurant, lies 400 metres down a side road.

Most of the many ventas around here have swimming pools. On summer weekends and weekday evenings half of Córdoba seeks the coolness of this area, cooking vast paellas in the many picnic spots. The ventas do roaring business. Weekday lunch times, however, are usually quiet and some establishments close on Mondays.

Make a detour up the Villaviciosa road and, through trees on your right, you glimpse a whitewashed mansion with a tower. This is Hacienda El Cordobés, the home of the so-called Beatle of the Bullring, the matador who became a national figure during the 1960s and 1970s. His rags-to-riches life story was consecrated in the book "Or I'll dress you in mourning".

Further on, amid rocky, pine-clad hills and the whirr of crickets, you find two more restaurants, El Oasis and Casa Pepe, and Las Jaras urbanisation overlooking a reservoir.

Returning to the Assuan restaurant junction, you can continue nine kilometres downhill to the city or turn eastwards, passing lofty antennae on your left. At a fork, swing left on CP45 into the Parque Periurbano Los Villares and towards Cerro Muriano. You pass a campsite and nature interpretation centre, then the Club de Campo, a sports complex with golf course.

A little further along is a large, shady picnic ground. The 484-hectare Parque Periurbano (literally "park on the periphery of the city"), the first of its type in Andalusia, aims to offer educational and recreational facilities while protecting nature. Oaks, chestnuts and pines cover this wilderness area.

At a T-junction, turn right towards Cerro Muriano and join the N432 that wriggles steeply downhill to return to Córdoba.

WHAT TO SEE

Panoramic views.

Madinat al-Zahra, open mid-Sept to April 10am-2pm, 4-6.30pm (May to mid-Sept open later pm), Sun 10am-2pm. Closed Mon.

Las Ermitas, open 10am-1.30pm, summer 5.30-8.45pm, winter 4.30-6 or 7pm. Closed Monday. Entry fee.

WHERE TO EAT

Any of the sierra restaurants. Barbecued meat is the speciality. Suggested: *Casa Pepe*, Ctra de Villaviciosa, km12.5. Tel: 957 73 90 50. Closed Mon lunch. Swimming pool. Try the *salmorejo*, typical Córdoba cold soup, and the revuelto de la casa.

WHERE TO STAY

Córdoba:

Córdoba is the obvious place to base yourself for this tour. The city has many hotels. The following are some recommendations.

Amistad Córdoba, Plaza Maimónides, 3. Tel. 957 42 03 35. Two 18th-century mansions adjoining the city wall converted into luxury hotel. Mudéjar patio. €€€€

Albucasis, Buen Pastor, 11. Tel: 957 47 86 25. Small, two-star hotel. Converted from old house near the Mosque. Large patio. €€.

Maestre, Romero Barros, 4. Tel. 957 47 24 10. Friendly one-star hotel near Plaza de Potro. €€

Next door is the two-star *Hostal Maestre* (tel. 957 47 53 95), a little cheaper. €

MORE INFORMATION

Córdoba:

Tourism office, Plaza Judá Leví, s/n. Tel: 957 20 05 22.
Open Mon-Fri 8.30am-2.30pm. Closed Sat, Sun.

Shrine to the Virgin, near Las Ermitas

Moorish palace at Madinat al-Zahra

Trout Streams
and
Renaissance Riches

Gorge on the Borosa River

HIDDEN AWAY IN ANDALUSIA'S NORTHEAST CORNER IS A WILDERNESS ZONE OF TUMBLING WATERFALLS, SOARING CRAGS, ABUNDANT WILDLIFE, AND REMOTE VILLAGES. TWO OF THE REGION'S BEST-PRESERVED HISTORIC TOWNS LIE ON THIS ROUTE.

PLAN A MINIMUM OF TWO TO THREE DAYS TO VISIT BAEZA, UBEDA AND THE CAZORLA NATURE PARK. IT IS IDEAL CAMPING COUNTRY, BUT THERE ARE COMFORTABLE HOTELS TOO. BRING YOUR BINOCULARS.

AREA: Jaén province
ROUTE: Jaén→Baeza→Ubeda→Cazorla→El Tranco→Segura →Jaén
DISTANCE: 440 kilometres

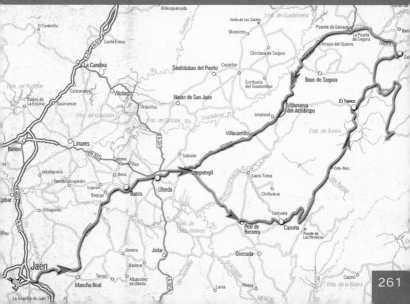

From Jaén, take the A316 towards Albacete. Regiments of olive trees march to the horizon for Jaén province produces some of Spain's finest olive oil. During the annual harvest from December to February, you will see pickers spreading sheets to collect the ripe fruit as it is shaken from the trees.

Olives must be crushed while fresh or a higher acid content results. The purest oil is *aceite virgen extra*, which has no additives or special treatment. La Casa del Aceite in Baeza (Paseo de la Constitución, 9) sells a selection of the finest oils.

After 48 kilometres you approach Baeza (pop. 16,000), a town of monuments, with an atmosphere, like its neighbour Ubeda, closer to that of sober Castile than flamenco-dancing Andalusia. Dating from Roman times, Baeza once ruled a Moorish mini-kingdom, but its most striking buildings date from the prosperous16th century.

Entering Baeza's quiet streets along the Camino Real, you encounter the Plaza del Pópulo, where the tourism office is housed in a fine Plateresque building. From its small projecting balcony the first mass was pronounced after the Moors were ousted, so tradition has it.

The adjacent Villalar Arch was built in 1521 to mark a victory over the Comuneros, a rebel movement in Castile. In the plaza centre is a fountain surmounted by an Iberian-Roman statue of a woman, said to be Imilce, wife of Hannibal.

Penetrating further into town, you come across the cathedral, a rich mixture of Gothic, Italian Renaissance and Mudéjar styles. Do not miss the ornate silver monstrance, revealed only after depositing a coin in a slot.

Just down the street is the impressive 15th-century Gothic Jabalquinto palace, with a beautiful patio and staircase. Opposite stands the noble Santa Cruz church, a rare example of Romanesque architecture.

A Renaissance building nearby housed a university for 300 years. Now a high school, it preserves the classroom where the great

Andalusian poet Antonio Machado taught French from 1912 to 1919. Machado lived on Plaza Cardenal Benavides opposite the Andalusian Plateresque town hall (as a wall plaque notes).

Up the road lies Ubeda (pop. 32,000), whose architectural magnificence justifies a leisurely visit. Ubeda owes much of its rich heritage to Francisco de los Cobos, a 16th-century wheeler-dealer who became the Emperor Charles V's secretary. His greed led to his downfall, and a relation, Juan Vázquez de Molina, replaced him.

Master architect Andrés de Vandelvira left a firm imprint on the town. His designs include Vázquez's palace, now the town hall, and the austere Hospital de Santiago, called "The Escorial of Andalusia".

Following signs along a bypass (or via a labyrinth of narrow, one-way streets), you reach the splendid Plaza Vázquez de Molina, with several Renaissance buildings. A 400-year-old palace which once accommodated Fernando Ortega Salido, first chaplain of the dazzling El Salvador chapel, now houses a parador.

Santa María de los Reales Alcázares, a 13th-century church built on the site of a mosque, has a beautiful cloister, but seems to be under permanent repair.

Shops sell local handicrafts, including the famed green pottery and esparto weavings, a tradition that goes back to Moorish times.

From Ubeda, take the N322 east, branching right at Torreperogil (which produces a very drinkable red wine) on the A315. You skirt cornfields and olive groves, crossing the Guadalquivir River at the Puente de la Cerrada reservoir and, at Peal de Becerro, turning left on the A319 to Cazorla.

As the sierras rear up ahead, you catch your first glimpse of Cazorla (pop. 9000), with a square watch tower standing guard above huddled dwellings. Gateway to the nature park, the town rambles up and down ridges at the foot of a crag called Los Halcones (the falcons).

Leave your car near the Plaza de la Constitución. Doctor Muñoz street (pedestrians only in the evenings) leads to the heart of Cazorla, the Plaza de la Corredera. Here you can enjoy excellent *tapas* at Las Vegas and La Montería bars. Squeezing down the older quarter's narrow streets and dodging traffic on José Salcedo Street, you arrive at the Plaza de Santa María.

Near the ruins of Santa María church, burned by Napoleon's troops, is the Cueva de Juan Pedro, a beamed, stone-walled restaurant which looks ancient enough to have welcomed Don Quixote for dinner.

Cazorla is the place to obtain information about the Parque Natural de Cazorla, Segura y Las Villas, Andalusia's largest nature park (214,000 hectares). Several enterprises offer horse treks and guided tours of the park with guides who are knowledgeable about the flora and fauna. Their four-wheel-drives can access tracks closed to other traffic.

From Cazorla the road runs past La Iruela, where the melodramatic Knights Templar castle clings to a crag. Any weapons you are carrying must be declared (permits are necessary to fish or hunt) at the park control point at Burunchel.

Zigzagging upwards, with vistas of olive-clad hills rolling to the horizon, you enter a pine and fir forest and at 1290 metres cross Las Palomas Pass. Stop at the first lookout point to get an idea of the extent of the park. It used to be known as the Mirador del Caudillo, recalling the time when the whole valley was sealed off so that General Franco could go hunting here.

The Guadalquivir valley runs northwards, bounded by thick forest (except where a disastrous fire scorched it in 2001) and bare mountain tops. Seventeen kilometres from Cazorla, you reach the Empalme del Valle, a crossroads with a large ceramic map of the park.

Continue straight ahead. Passing a turn to the right to the magnificently situated Parador El Adelantado, you curve down to the Guadalquivir River.

Here you can make a pleasant 30-to-40-minute walk, following the path which leads downriver through a spectacular chasm. Water foams over a dam, then you reach the Linarejos waterfall, a fine sight in years of good rains as it tumbles over a rock face. Continue on the path, circling around to meet the road again.

Back in the car, cross the river-bridge and turn immediately right towards the source of the Guadalquivir. After three kilometres, just after a privately-run camp-ground, you cross the Puente de las Herrerías. Legend has it that this bridge was built in one night so that Queen Isabel could speed past en route to conquer the Moorish Kingdom of Granada.

From the bridge, an unpaved track winds 12 kilometres up the valley to La Cañada de las Fuentes, where the Guadalquivir bubbles from beneath a rock and begins its 660-kilometre journey to the Atlantic. You can continue through the mountains for another 24 kilometres to bring you back to La Iruela.

Near the Guadalquivir source you can also take the track to Pozo Alcón, which winds up through pinewoods until you pass near the summit of Cabañas, a bare 2000-metre peak.

Here as elsewhere in the park you may see circling eagles and hawks. Peonies, lupins, orchids and the unique Cazorla violet bloom in springtime. Fallow and red deer, muflón (mountain sheep), wild goats, boar, fox and badger are common. Be careful driving at night as deer often stray on to the roads.

The easiest way to view the larger animals is to visit the viewing point called the Parque Cinegético in early morning and near sunset. Fodder and water are provided to attract the animals.

To reach that area, return to the Empalme del Valle and take the road down the valley towards El Tranco. The animals' feeding-point is about 32 kilometres from the Empalme.

Before that you reach the Torre del Vinagre interpretation centre, which has useful information on the park's geology, plants and animals, though the colour photos badly need replacing.

Autumn in Sierra de Segura

Next door is a hunting museum, with a daunting range of trophies. Among these are the horns of stags that died of starvation when their horns locked during the autumn battles for supremacy. One of Franco's record trophies is displayed, dated 1958, but his name has mysteriously disappeared. When he came to fish and shoot, he stayed at the solid stone lodge next to the museum. Nearby is a botanical garden.

One of the most delightful walks starts nearby. It's quite an easy one. Take the road opposite the Torre del Vinagre across the river and park beyond the Piscifactoría. At this hatchery, thousands of rainbow trout eggs from Canada are raised for stocking local rivers.

A track, closed to traffic, runs alongside the Borosa River to a hydro-electric station. Follow this route up the valley. Trout frolic in the clear tumbling river. Lizards skitter away at your approach. If you trek three to four hours, the last section up a steep gulch of tumbled rocks, you reach the lakes of Aguas Negras and Valdeazores.

Less energetic types can limit themselves to a three-hour round trip. Where the track veers away from the river, stick to the path towards Cerrada de Elías. It crosses foot bridges over cascading water, then reaches a narrow gorge where wooden planks are pinned to the rock face. Shortly after, the path meets the track again.

Campsites, picnic spots and ventas dot the road to El Tranco. Several new hotels have sprung up. During school holidays and weekends, the number of visitors frightens off much of the wild life in the valley.

El Tranco dam, 90 metres high, is designed to retain up to 500 million cubic metres of water. Once across the dam, you can cut short the trip by turning sharp left to descend westwards alongside the river towards Villanueva del Arzobispo.

Alternatively, continue on A319 towards wild and windy Hornos (pop. 800), high on a crag with a ruined castle. Park by the town hall and the medieval Asunción parish church. A doorway alongside the town hall leads to the Mirador El Aguilón, from where you gaze down on the valley and El Tranco reservoir.

Allow at least three hours round trip if from here you plan to visit the source of the Segura River. The A317 to Pontones corkscrews up through the forest before emerging on a ridge with tremendous vistas of cliffs, crags and distant lake. It descends near some odd rock formations to the dozing settlement of Pontones.

Turn right just after the village to Fuente Segura. A track runs five kilometres to a picnic spot and a point where chill, transparent water surges from a blue grotto. This is the Río Segura, which eventually empties into the Mediterranean in Murcia.

Retracking, continue on the route that runs below Hornos from El Tranco towards Puente de Génave and turn right to Segura de la Sierra (pop. 300), so dramatically situated at 1200 metres above sea level it looks like a film set.

Visigoths, Moors and Christians all made use of this strongpoint. Peer from the ramparts of the much-restored castle and be glad you don't have to lay siege to it. En route to the castle, note the unusual plaza de toros, rectangular and partly chipped out of rock.

Opposite the town hall stands a statue of Jorge Manrique, a revered 15th-century poet born here or nearby. Across the valley towers the crag of El Yelmo. A favourite launch site for hang-gliders and paragliders, it can be reached by road.

Segura is a good centre for exploring the remoter parts of the park, though snow and ice can make the backroads hazardous in winter. From Segura it is 24 kilometres via Orcera and La Puerta de Segura to Puente de Génave on the N322. A left takes you back via Ubeda to Jaén.

WHAT TO SEE

Baeza:

Cathedral, open 1.30am-1pm, 5-7pm (4-6pm in winter). Closed Wed.

Jabalquinto Palace, undergoing repairs.

Vera-Cruz Museum, open 11am-1.30pm, 4.30-7pm (July-Aug mornings only). Statues, floats of religious order founded 1540.

Universidad Antigua (Old University), open 10am-2pm, 4-6pm (call 953 74 01 74 first).

Ubeda:

Capilla del Salvador, open 10.30am-2pm, 4.30-6pm. Entry 2€. Renaissance gem.

Hospital de Santiago, open 8am-3pm, 3.30-10pm.

Casa de las Torres, open 8am-2.30pm, 4-6pm. 16th-century Plateresque palace. *Museo de Alfarería* (pottery museum), Plaza Vázquez de Molina. Open 10.30am-2pm, 5.30-8pm. Closed Sun pm, Mon. Entry 1.80 euros.

Museo Arqueológico, Cervantes, 6. Open Tues-Sat 9am-8pm. Closed Sun pm, Mon. *Museo de San Juán de la Cruz*, Carmen, s/n. Includes cell where the mystic died. Open: 11am-12.45pm, 5-6.45pm. Closed Mon.

Cazorla:

Museo del Alto Guadalquivir, Castillo La Yedra. Tel. 953-71 00 39. Open Sun 9am-3pm, Tues 3-8pm, Wed-Sat 9am-8pm. Closed Mon. Spectacularly situated folk museum, weapons, artefacts.

Nature park, *Torre del Vinagre* (Ctra del Tranco km18) flora and fauna exhibition, hunting museum.

Piscifactoría, near Torre del Vinagre. Open 11am-2pm, 4-6pm. Closed Mon, Tues. Trout hatchery.

Segura de la Sierra:

Arab baths.

Castle, always open.

Bullring.

Jesuits' church (under restoration).

16th-century fountain.

WHERE TO STAY

Baeza:

Baeza, Concepción, 3, tel. 953 74 81 30. Modern three-star hotel €€€

Hospedería Fuentenueva, Paseo Arca del Agua. Tel. 953 74 31 00. Welcoming 12-room hotel in ex-women's prison. €€€

Ubeda:

Parador, Plaza Vázquez de Molina, 1. Tel. 953 75 03 45. 16th-century mansion €€€-€€€€.

Palacio de la Rambla, Plaza del Marqués, 1. Tel. 953 75 01 96. Closed mid-July to mid-August. Aristocratic splendour in Renaissance mansion. Antique furnishings. €€€.

María de Molina, Plaza del Ayuntamiento. Tel. 953 79 53 56. Closed mid-July-mid-Aug. Comfortable rooms in mansion, splendid patio. €€€

Cazorla:

Finca Mercedes, Ctra de la Sierra, km1, La Iruela. Tel. 953 72 10 87. Welcoming comfortable family-run hotel. Hearty meals. €

Villa Turística, Ladera de San Isicio. Tel. 953 71 01 00. Village complex, heating, cooking facilities, pool, restaurant. €€€

Parador El Adelantado, Ctra de la Sierra, Nature park. Tel. 953 72 70 75. Closed Dec 9-Feb 1. Amid scenic grandeur. Lawns, swimming pool. Recommended restaurant. €€€

La Hortizuela, Ctra del Tranco, km18.5. Tel. 953 71 31 50. Closed Jan-mid-Feb. Comfortable, tranquil. Pool. €-€€

Noguera de la Sierpe, Ctra de la Sierra, Km 13, Coto Ríos. Tel: 953 71 30 21. Stuffed lion, African safari trophies set the tone. Riding, boating, swimming pool. Half pension only. €€€€ (2 persons).

El Pinar, Ctra del Tranco, km20. Tel 953 71 30 68. Apartments sleeping 4-8. Restaurant, excellent local dishes. €€

Albergue Universitario Jorge Manrique, Francisco de Quevedo, 1, Segura de la Sierra. Tel. 953-48 04 14. Aimed at sporting, educational, ecology groups. Six comfortable en suite double rooms. Ultra-friendly staff. Budget restaurant. €

WHERE TO EAT

Baeza:

Vandelvira, San Francisco, 14. Tel. 953 74 81 72. Closed Sun night & Mon. Former convent, with glassed-in cloister; *Juanito*, Paseo Arca del Agua, s/n. Tel: 953 74 00 40. Closed Sun, Mon nights. Noted for regional dishes. Service can be off-hand. *Hospedería Fuentenueva* serves traditional food.

La Góndola, Portales Carbonería, 13. Tel. 953-74 29 84. Cosy bar for tapas.

Ubeda:

Restaurants of the Parador, Palacio de La Rambla and *María de Molina* hotels. *El Gallo Rojo*, Torrenueva, 3. Tel. 953 75 20 38. Good value local dishes.

Mesón Navarro, Plaza del Ayuntamiento, 2. Tel. 953 79 06 38. Excellent for tapas.

Cazorla:

Cueva de Juan Pedro & Asador Plaza Vieja, Plaza Santa María. Tel: 953 72 12 25. Antonio and Chelo run these friendly restaurants. Roast boar, venison.

Villa Turística restaurant, regional dishes.

Nature park:

Hostal Mirasierra, Ctra del Tranco Km 20, Coto Ríos. Tel: 953 72 05 00. Grilled trout.

El Mirador de Mesía de Leiva, Postigo, 2, Segura de la Sierra. Tel. 953 48 21 01. Agreeable bar/restaurant. Try scrambled eggs with asparagus and shrimps.

MORE INFORMATION

Baeza:
Tourism office, Plaza del Pópulo. Tel. 953 74 04 44.
Open: 9am-2pm, 5-7.30pm. Closed Sat, Sun.

Ubeda:
Tourism office, Palacio Marqués de Contadero, Baja del Marqués, 4.
Tel. 953 75 08 97. Open: 8am-7pm, Sat-Sun 10am-2pm.

Cazorla:
Tourism office, Paseo Santo Cristo, 17. Tel. 953 71 01 02. Open
Mon-Fri mornings. Closed Oct-March;

Cazorla Nature Park:
Centro de Interpretación, Torre del Vinagre, Ctra del Tranco km18.
Tel. 953 72 01 15. Open 11am-2pm, 4-6pm, later in summer.
Closed Mon.

Oficina del Parque Natural, Martínez Falero, 11, Cazorla.
Tel. 953 72 01 25. Open Mon-Fri 8am-2.30pm. Fishing, hunting
permits, park technical details. Not for tourist information;

Quercus, Juan Domingo, 2 Cazorla. Tel: 953 72 01 15. Excursions
and guides. Excursiones Cazorla, Ctra de la Siera, La Iruela.
Tel. 639 99 35 45.

Segura village and castle

Fiestas

Passing through Doñana nature reserve en route to El Rocío

ANDALUSIA'S FIESTAS OFFER A GREAT EXPERIENCE. EXUBERANT, COLOURFUL, FULL OF VITALITY AND MUSIC . . . THEY WILL LIVE IN YOUR MEMORY. AND THERE ARE HUNDREDS TO CHOOSE FROM. HOWEVER, IF YOU CAN'T STAND CROWDS, HIGH DECIBELS AND TRAFFIC JAMS, YOU MAY NOT BE SO ENTHUSIASTIC.

Fiestas are not the ideal time to do the sights. Shops and public buildings are closed, churches and other monuments difficult to visit. Hotels are fully booked. Also if the fiesta is close to a weekend, many Spaniards take the chance to make excursions so that there may be extra traffic on the roads.

Every town and village has an annual *feria* (fair), several days when little work is done and entertainment usually includes bullfights, fireworks, flamenco dancing and fairground fun, plus a certain amount of drinking. *Romerías* consist of a pilgrimage to a local religious shrine, followed by flamenco, dancing and drinking.

For fiesta fans and seekers after tranquillity, here is a brief rundown of the bigger sprees and some interesting smaller ones. Note dates can vary so check them with local tourist offices or town halls.

CELEBRATED REGION-WIDE

Cabalgata de Reyes, January 5 The Three Kings arrive on this night, bearing gifts for the children. Colourful processions parade through towns and cities, the Kings sometimes mounted on camels.

Carnival, in February an excuse for a big party. Fancy dress dances and big parades are held all over Andalusia before and after Ash Wednesday, but it is in Cádiz where the celebrations really go over the top. Satirical ditties poking fun at well-known personalities are sung by competing groups.

Semana Santa A mixture of solemn pomp and pagan ecstasy characterises Holy Week, celebrated in every town and village. Processions, the biggest in Seville and Málaga, begin on Palm Sunday and reach a climax on Good Friday.

Corpus Christi (May or June) Many towns decorate the streets for the solemn procession. It is particularly worth seeing in Granada where *La Tarasca*, a figure mounted on a dragon's back, and bigheads parade through town.

Virgen del Carmen On July 15 or 16, fishermen pay homage to their patron in numerous towns, including Barbate (Cádiz), Estepona, Málaga, Nerja, Salobreña (Granada) and Garrucha (Almeria). The Virgin's image is taken for a sea voyage amid popular acclamation.

LOCAL FIESTAS OF INTEREST

Almería Annual fair, last week of August. Homage is paid to the Virgin of the Sea.

Andújar (Jaén province), last weekend in April, **Romería to la Virgen de la Cabeza**.

Baza (Granada), **El Cascamorras**, September 6. Annual fair starting with the attempt by the *Cascamorras*, a representative of neighbouring Guadix, to recover a disputed Virgin. Dirty liquid is poured over him and he is chased through the town.

Córdoba Patios Festival, first fortnight of May. Patios are opened to the public for this event that includes concerts and flamenco. The Córdoba fair is held in the second half of May.

El Rocío (Huelva), Pentecost (May or early June). Andalusia's most popular fiesta attracts a million or so people. They trek to a sanctuary near the mouth of the Guadalquivir, to pay homage to the *Virgen del Rocío*, whose image is paraded from the early hours of a Monday morning.

Granada **Día de la Toma**, January 2. Solemn procession through the city streets to celebrate the 1492 victory of the Catholic

Monarch over the Moorish Kingdom of Granada; May 3, **Day of the Cross**, colourful spring festival; May, **International Theatre Festival**; End of June, **International Music and Dance Festival**.

Huelva **Columbus fiesta**, first week of August.

Jerez **Feria del Caballo**, first week of May. Flamenco, equestrian competitions, bullfights and a certain amount of sherry drinking. Jerez holds its wine festival for two weeks leading up to the **Día de la Merced**, September 24.

Málaga Fair, first two weeks of August. Businesses close early as Málaga does its best to outdo the Seville Fair; December 28, **Fiesta of the Verdiales**, a primitive, driving music dating at least from Moorish times, held just outside town at the **Venta de San Cayetano**; Puerto de la Torre.

Ronda (Málaga), **Pedro Romero Fiesta**, first fortnight of September. A **Corrida Goyesca** is held, bullfighters wearing dress typical of Goya's time.

Sanlúcar de Barrameda, **Manzanilla Wine Fair**, mid-May; **Exaltación al Río Guadalquivir**, mid-August; horse races on the beach, second and fourth week August.

Seville Fair (usually in April) A very public private party lasting a whole week, with daily parade through the fairgrounds, from around midday, of horsemen and carriages, bullfights and non-stop flamenco. Beds are hard to find.

REGIONAL HOLIDAYS

The following are holidays all over Andalusia (in addition, towns have local holidays) New Year's Day; January 6, **Día de los Reyes**; February 28, **Día de Andalucía**; Easter Thursday, Good Friday (Easter Monday is not a holiday); May 1, **Labour Day**; May/June; **Corpus Christi** (not observed in all localities); August 15, **Assumption of the Virgin**; October 12, National Day or **Día del Pilar**; November 1, **All Saints' Day;** December 6, **Day of the Constitution**; December 8, **Immaculate Conception; Christmas Day.**

VOCABULARY AND USEFUL PHRASES

ON THE ROAD

Is there a petrol station near here? - *¿Hay una gasolinera (or estación de servicio) por aquí?*

Fill her up, please - *Lleno, por favor*

Where is the road to Seville? - *¿Dónde está la carretera para Sevilla?*

How do I get to the airport, the market? - *¿Como se puede ir al aeropuerto, al mercado?*

Left - *Izquierda.*

Right - *Derecha.*

Straight on - *todo recto*

First right/second left - *la primera a la derecha, la segunda a la izquierda.*

To turn left - *girar a la izquierda.*

Crossroads - *cruce.*

Traffic lights - *semáforos.*

Diesel - *gasoil.*

Driving licence - *carnet de conducir.*

Insurance certificate - *certificado de seguro.*

Logbook - *cartilla de propiedad.*

Mechanic - *mecánico.*

Oil - *aceite.*

Petrol - *gasolina* (lead-free - *sin plomo*).

Petrol station - *gasolinera.*

Puncture - *pinchazo.*

Repair shop - *taller de reparaciones or garaje.*

ROAD SIGNS

Aparcamiento - parking

Autovía - four-lane highway

Autopista - motorway, turnpike (toll may be payable)

Carga o descarga - Loading and unloading zone, no parking

Carretera cortada - road blocked

Ceda el paso - give way

Centro urbano - town centre

Circunvalación, ronda - bypass

Entrada - entrance

Firme en mal estado - poor road surface

Llamamos grua - We call the tow-truck (i.e. no parking)

Peaje - toll to pay

Peatones - pedestrians

Peligro - danger

Prohibido aparcar, no aparcar - parking forbidden

Prohibido el paso - no entry

Salida - exit

Tramo en obras - road works

Vado permanente - entrance always in use

Vado inundable - subject to flooding

Vía única - one way

BREAKDOWNS

I have run out of petrol - *Me he quedado sin gasolina*

I have a puncture (flat battery) - *Tengo un neumático pinchado (la batería descargada)*

My car has broken down - *Mi coche está averiado*

The car will not start - *El coche no arranca*

The lights don't work - *No funcionan los faros*

I need a tow-truck - *necesito la grua*

Where is the nearest garage? - *¿Dónde está el taller de coches más cerca?*

Can you fix it? - *¿Puede arreglarlo?*

Do you do repairs? - *¿Hace reparaciones?*

Battery - *batería*

Brakes - *frenos*

Bulb - *bombilla*

car keys - *llaves del coche*

clutch - *embrague*

distilled water - *agua destilada*

exhaust - *escape*

fan belt - *correa de ventilador*

fuse - *fusible*

gearbox - *caja de cambios*

headlights - *faros*

petrol tank - *depósito de gasolina*

points - *contactos*

radiator - *radiador*

seat-belts - *cinturones de seguridad*

spark plug - *bujía*

tyre - *neumático*

wheel - *rueda* (spare wheel - *rueda de recambio*)

windscreen - *parabrisas*

EMERGENCIES

ambulancia - ambulance

casa de socorro, puesto de socorro - first aid post

comisaría de policía - police station

Cruz Roja - Red Cross

cuartel de la Guardia Civil - Civil Guard post

farmacia - chemist, pharmacy

hospital, sanitario - hospital

médico - doctor

urgencias - casualty department

I am lost - *Me he perdido*

There's been an accident - *Ha ocurrido un accidente*

I have been robbed - *He sido robado* or *me han robado*

Call the police - *Llama a la policía*

I have lost my luggage, my passport, the car keys, my wife - *He perdido mi equipaje, mi pasaporte, las llaves del coche, mi mujer*

I am ill - *Estoy enfermo/a* (adjectives end in "*a*" when applied to women)

I need a doctor, a dentist, a lawyer - *Necesito un médico, un dentista, un abogado*

I am diabetic, pregnant - *Soy diabético/a, estoy embarazada*

I have heart trouble - *Estoy del corazón*

USEFUL BASICS

Please - *Por favor*

Thank you - *Gracias*

Good morning - *Buenos días*

Good afternoon - *Buenas tardes*

Good night - *Buenas noches*

Goodbye - *Adiós* or *Hasta luego*

Where is the post office, railway station, police station? - *¿Dónde está la oficina de correos, la estación de ferrocarril, la comisaría?*

Where is the toilet? - *¿Dónde están los servicios* (also *caballeros* and *damas*)?

Where can I buy a film, postcards, cigarettes, stamps, medicine? - *¿Dónde puedo comprar una película, postales, tobaco, sellos, medicina?*

Do you have a room free? - *¿Hay una habitación libre?*

I would like a double (single) room - *Querría una habitación doble (individual).*

Can I see the menu? - *¿Puedo ver la carta?*

I like the food - *Me gusta la comida*

Breakfast - *Desayuno*

Lunch - *Almuerzo*

Dinner - *Cena*

How much is it? - *¿Cuánto es?*

The bill, please - *La cuenta, por favor*

What time is it? - *¿Qué hora es?*

It is two o'clock, midnight - *Son las dos, es medianoche.*

When does the bus to Estepona leave? - *¿A qué hora sale el autobús para Estepona?*

What time does the plane from London arrive? - *¿A qué hora llega el vuelo de Londres?*

COMMONLY USED SPANISH WORDS

abierto - open

aficionado - amateur, fan (sport)

autobús or *autocar* (long distance) - bus

ayer - yesterday

ayuntamiento, casa consistorial - town hall

balneario - spa

barrio - quarter (of a town)

bodega - wine cellar

calle - street

cama - bed

cambiar - to change

campo - countryside, field

carretera - highway

cerrado - closed

cerveza - beer

ciudad - city

coche - car

comida - meal

corrida - bullfight

cortijo - farmhouse

dinero - money
finca - farm
fino - dry sherry
gitano - gypsy
hoy - today
jamón serrano - mountain-cured ham
mañana - tomorrow
mañana por la mañana - tomorrow morning
mercado - market
mesón - bar-restaurant
mirador - viewpoint
moto - motor-cycle
pan - bread
parador - state-run hotel
playa - beach
plaza - square
pueblo - village, town
tablao flamenco - night club
tapa - snack
venta - inn

ARCHITECTURE

alcazaba - castle
alcázar - fortress, royal palace
artesonado - Moorish-style coffered ceiling
azulejo - glazed tile
barroco - Baroque, ornate style
capilla mayor - chapel with high altar
claustro - cloister
churrigueresco - Churrigueresque, highly ornate Baroque art
coro - chancel with choir-stalls

ermita - hermitage

isabelino - Isabelline, Gothic style from era of Queen Isabel

mihrab - prayer niche in a mosque

mozárabe - Mozarab, art developed by Christians under Moslem rule

mudéjar - Moslem art in Christian-occupied territory

murallas - walls, ramparts

neo-clásico - Neo-classical, imitating sober Greek and Roman styles

plateresco - Plateresque, finely carved early Renaissance style

qibla - mosque wall orientated towards Mecca

reja - iron grille

retablo - decorated altarpiece

torre del homenaje - keep

0, *cero*

1, *uno*

2, *dos*

3, *tres*

4, *cuatro*

5, *cinco*

6, *seis*

7, *siete*

8, *ocho*

9, *nueve*

10, *diez*

20, *veinte*

25, *veinticinco*

50, *cincuenta*

100, *cien*

500, *quinientos*

1,000, *mil*

INDEX

For a full list of our
essential books on Spain contact:
Santana Books,
Apartado 422,
29640 Fuengirola (Málaga) Spain.
Tel: 952 485 838. Fax: 952 485 367.
E-mail: sales@santanabooks.com
www.santanabooks.com

UK Representatives
Aldington Books Ltd.,
Unit 3(b) Frith Business Centre,
Frith Road, Aldington,
Ashford, Kent TN25 7HJ.
Tel: 01233 720 123. Fax: 01233 721 272
E-mail: sales@aldingtonbooks.co.uk
www.aldingtonbooks.co.uk